NOBBUT MIl ____
Laugh with the Dalesfolk

by W R Mitchell

CASTLEBERG
2000

A niggardly grocer: *He'd nip a currant in two.*

A wealthy farmer: *He's bow-legged wi' brass.*

A peevish child: *She's as twined as a wasp.*

An awkward person: *He's bad to shave.*

Of a long-haired youth: *If tha goes bi t'barber's shop, pole'll drop.*

Said a farm-man on a low wage: *I wark accordin'.*

Of a strong cup o' tea: *As hot as hell an' as black as t'fireback.*

Of a domesticated husband: *He's as handy as t'dish-clout.*

A farmer's dance: *They were just like a lot o' bullocks gone wild.*

A Dales social evening: *It were grand; we had t'piano ower three times.*

Drawings:
   Richard Bancroft
Photography:
   W R Mitchell
Front cover:
   IONICUS (colouring by Malcolm Hunter)

NOBBUT MIDDLIN'
Laugh with the Dalesfolk

Contents

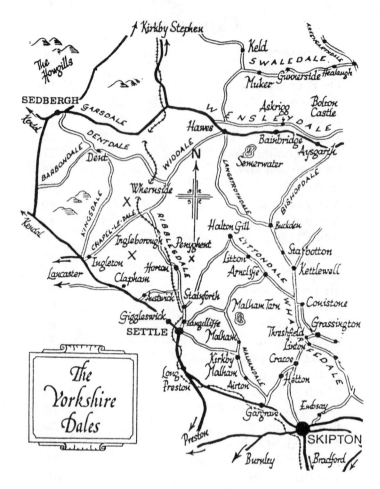

A **Castleberg** Book.

First published in the United Kingdom in 2000.

Text, © W R Mitchell 2000.

The moral right of the author has been asserted.

ISBN 1 871064 39 2

Typeset in New Baskerville, printed and bound in the United Kingdom by Lamberts Print & Design, Station Road, Settle, North Yorkshire, BD24 9AA.

Published by Castleberg, 18 Yealand Avenue, Giggleswick, Settle, North Yorkshire, BD24 0AY.

Introduction
or Let's Git Started...

Judge the health of those who live in the Yorkshire Dales by the colour of their faces. If it's ashen, it's a bad colour. Summat must be done about it. Daleheaders didn't bother much wi' doctors, who had a nasty habit of charging for their services. It was cheaper to die naturally.

A florid face signifies high blood pressure – or, at the dalehead, the beginnings of rust. A dalesman with a good colour [pinkish] is said to be *nobbut middlin'*, as well as can be expected. You can discount twinges [rheumatics] which are endemic in a dampish atmosphere. A native of the Dales will never admit that all's well, but with "a good colour" he's nowt much to complain about. Except, that is, Owd Jack, who looked mournful while admitting that his hay crop had been good and "them taties" couldn't have been better. "Then what's up wi' thee?" demanded his friend. "Nay," said Jack, "ivvery time I think about hay and taties, I worry about all t'goodness they've takken out of t'ground."

A Wharfedale farmer, when asked how he was, would go no further than: "I'se all reight – in health." Some dalesfolk are *caingy* or *tetchy* [bad-tempered]. When I inquired about the age of a chap in Nidderdale, he said: "I'se eighty-five." I attempted to flatter him by remarking; "You don't look eighty-five." He snapped: "Can't help that!" Then you get the type who's *kysty* [fastidious]. He picks at his food instead of getting it eaten. One farm man who was prospecting with his dinner fork sounded a bit peevish when he said: "It looks as though t'dumplings have etten all t'meat."

As the years roll by, a dalesman/woman might become *maffly* [muddled or forgetful]. The nonagenarian who was dying said, haltingly, when his wife and relatives were present in his bedroom: "Don't forget – Benjamin owes us five pounds." His wife beamed at the thought. The old chap stirred again and said: "And don't forget we owe Jonathan ten pounds." Said the wife, shaking her head sadly: "Poor chap – he's maffly." When an old-time dalesman was in t'mood for talk – and that wasn't often – there was no stopping him. Hearing that in the Cowling area, just off Airedale, the red grouse quack, not crow, I went to investigate and came upon a chatty freeholder who had shooting rights, "for nowt," on Kornsher [Ickornshaw] Moor. It was a treat to listen to him. The freehold territory lay beside tracts of moor owned by t'gentry, who employed gamekeepers and beaters. The freeholders claimed any avian refugees that skimmed the walls on to their territory.

Asked about quacking grouse, the old chap remarked: "When it's just brekkin' light, grouse start a-crowing to one another. And that's what we call t'quack." He said of the moor itself: "There's plenty o' watter on it and bits o' foot tracks 'at folks have made." The gentry had well-made butts. The Cowling men made use of any cover they could cobble together. I heard about Mucky Dyke butt, which was "sludgy," and the rather more fashionable King's Seat, though I reckon that if a king had decided to sit there he'd be recommended to don his fustian breeches to ward off the damp.

When a Wensleydale farmer who was "under the weather" consulted a doctor, a change of climate was recommended. "Nay," said the ailing man, "I've nivver had nowt else – living in Hawes all mi life." Charlie Lawson, of Settle, related how a young man on his honeymoon sat looking out of the bedroom window, gazing at the sky. His bride invited him to come to bed. He said: "Nay – my mother said this would be the most wonderful night of mi life. I'm not going to miss one minute of it."

Bouncing Babies

There she was - a district nurse, in her smart blue outfit, neat cap and black bag, using a track beside a wood on her way to deliver a baby at a remote farm, when the silence was not so much broken as shattered by a screaming sound. At the farm, she mentioned that murder must have been committed in the wood. "Nay," said the farmer, "it's nobbut a vixen fox on heat."

The district nurse of years ago had usually trained as a midwife. Most children were born at home, not in hospital. Large families were the rule. Parents might resort to the Bible when seeking names for the youngest children. One lad was given the name Hobadiah but was, in his long life, referred to as "our 'Ob'." Mr and Mrs Hoyle might have given the matter of naming their daughter more thought before calling her Olive. And why did they send the husband to register the birth of his daughter Helen? He was in the habit of dropping aitches and she was officially recorded as Ellen.

In Swaledale, where Aldersons proliferated, nicknames were the rule and the child who grew up to become William Alderson, JP, retained throughout his life the name Gurt Bill. When an Austwick couple had their child christened Bill, the vicar observed it was not a good name for a baby. Said the mother: "He won't always be a baby."

A woman in labour needed experienced help. And who was more experienced than Nanny or Owd Betty? These were the nicknames of daleswomen who were excellent midwives before it became a profession. Nanny, a woman living in a Craven dale, was also summoned to any sickly animals. Owd Betty's domain was upper Swaledale, where it was said: "Nobody paid her for deliverin' t'bairns; they'd just get her a bit of a present. She was really mad if she wasn't asked."

If, in the Keasden area, a family expecting "a happy event" could not get in touch with a nurse or doctor, they summoned Grannie Swindlehurst to help out. Granny had a bevy of children of her own. She was soon demanding copious quantities of boiling water, both for sterilisation purposes and to provide the worried husband with some occupational therapy. Grannie never allowed herself to get over-excited. When she had assisted the child into the world, and the child had the customary "boiled lobster" appearance, it was only a matter of minutes before the nearest and dearest were trying to decide from facial details which side of the family had been favoured. "I think he/she favours his/her mother," someone would remark. A baby was never allowed to be him/herself.

A doctor with a rural round employed a coachman for his horse and trap. Help was needed to open the many gates and to attend to the horse while the doctor was delivering the baby. One snowtime, a Skipton doctor rode on horseback to a remote farm and, the child being not yet ready, he slept on the sofa in the front room. It was said of a doctor who shall be unnamed that he was so slow in responding to a call to a heavily pregnant woman that when he arrived the child had been born and was almost ready for school. "Churching" was general. A new mother would not dream of visiting another house until she had been to church to thank God for a safe delivery.

Norah Johnson, who became a district nurse, also trained as a midwife. In 1939, while in the Barnard Castle district, she had some "rare trips" through a snowbound landscape. Norah drove a car; her colleague, who could not drive, took the jobs near at hand, for she rode a bike.

When Norah was summoned in snowtime to a birth on the Strathmore estate at Holwick in Teesdale, she had to leave her car at the roadside and cross a beck. At a farm, she delivered twins. As she was about to leave, the farmer brought her a horse and said that when she reached her car she must just turn the horse round and it would return home on its own account.

At another farm, Norah sterilised and set up her equipment and placed the swabs, which she had boiled, on the shiny fender of the farm kitchen. The baby's bath was ready for use. Without warning, a lump of ceiling and an assortment of bugs, fell into the sterile bowl. Early in her career, while attending to a confinement in Shropshire, she had been assisted by an old Grannie who was so strung up that when she came to pour some hot water into the basin, as Norah attended to the baby, most of the water flowed through one of the midwife's shoes. "Poor thing – she didn't know what she was doing." A gurgling noise at a farm turned out to be from cider production in the cellar.

She returned to the Dales in 1945. "I used to say that I'd looked all round Shropshire for a farmer and didn't find one so I came back to the Dales as a nurse at Settle. I was here eighteen months when I met Emanuel Johnson. So I got my Yorkshire farmer. During the twenty months she was nursing in the Dales before her marriage, she delivered almost a hundred babies. Two nurses were maintained for the Settle area, the area extending from town to Ribblehead, Keasden and Tosside. "We delivered all the babies then. One of us might stay up all night to attend a birth, return home, have an hour's sleep and wake in time to go on the morning rounds."

There were times when nature took its course unattended by a nurse. At a farm near Stainforth, the baby was BBA – baby born on arrival – and Norah found it on the bed. It was the third child and had come quickly. The farmer had done what was necessary. There was an ante natal clinic in St John's hall. The nurses also visited pregnant women at their homes. "We delivered the babies – and later attended to them as the school nurse."

The most demanding time was in the early months of 1947 when blizzards reshaped the contours of the landscape. The road from Settle to Skipton was blocked by snow for two days, which created problems when she had to attend to an expectant mother at Merebeck. Norah telephoned the police, who were unable to help but suggested that she rang up the railway station. The stationmaster arranged for a light engine to be drawn up on the stretch of line adjacent to the bottom of Norah's garden on the Ingfield Estate.

She was assisted over the fence and on to the footplate of the engine, being taken to a point near Merebeck, where the stationmaster helped her, complete with bag, up a snowy bank. She crossed some fields to reach the house where she delivered a baby. As she returned to Settle on foot at about 6-30 a.m., Norah met some RAF men who were digging snow. "They wondered where the dickens I had come from." That same winter, she was called to a wooden structure at Helwith Bridge where a couple were in temporary occupation. The police drove her to the expectant mother, though not by the direct way. They crossed Buckhaw Brow and went by Wharfe. The police waited while she delivered the baby and then brought Norah home again.

Dr Jane O'Connor, who with her husband bought a practice at Settle in 1933, found the dalesfolk shy and reserved. Eventually, the women were confiding in her but some of the men were not so sure. An elderly man with bronchitis asked the doctor: "Are you married?" "Yes." "Is your husband alive?" "Yes." Only then did he allow the doctor to look at his chest.

Jane O'Connor took over the practice when her husband joined the RAF. She was called out to a remote cottage where an evacuee from a big city had cut her buttock. She had been using a chamber pot, to which she was not accustomed, when it broke; hence the injury. The doctor, having driven to the house at night using only the sidelights of the car, had to stitch up the injury by candlelight. (On the following day, the mother collected her daughter and they returned to the city).

When a Dales farming couple had their first baby, the wife went upstairs one evening and saw her husband standing by the cot, looking at it hard and long. The wife, touched by the sight, her eyes filling with tears, put her arms around him. He stared at the touch. Said the wife: "Now then, Jack, what are you thinking?" He replied: "How we managed to get a good cot like that for only five pounds."

A Dales farmer yearns for a son and then he cannot wait until the baby has grown into a lad who is useful about the place. The father of six children waited patiently for the schooldays to pass and rejoiced when yet another child left school and was able to become a full-time worker. When the last of the six was freed from what he was inclined to think as the shackles of education, someone remarked: "How does it feel now tha's gitten all thi pullets layin'?"

On Four Wheels

In little more than a lifetime, the "infernal" combustion engine has ousted horse traffic, transformed our lives and cluttered up the Dales. At the edge of living memory, most farmers biked or used t'bus when going to market. More recently, when a farmer took delivery of a new car to replace the "old banger" that had served him for years, he took the newcomer back to the garage and said: "It's not rattlin' reight."

When I first explored the Dales, over fifty years ago, motor vehicles were spaced on the road at intervals of about twenty minutes, which was hard luck if I had missed a bus and needed to "thumb" a lift. Now traffic is almost bumper to bumper and on languid days the air reeks of oil. A familiar summer sight is that of sunlight gleaming on lines of parked cars at Dales "honeypots" such as Aysgarth, Kettlewell or beside the Wharfe near Bolton Abbey.

In the pioneering days of motoring, the road was waterbound and people dressed for motoring, in some cases sitting behind a gigantic windscreen which was also a dust screen. A Hawes man, knocked down by one of the first cars to penetrate the region, was picked up and dusted down by the driver. Was he injured? "Nay – there's nowt that wean't mend." What would he like in the way of compensation? The dalesman thought for a moment, then asked; "What does ta usually pay?"

My knowledge of early motoring in the Dales was built up partly through chats with Fred Ellis, of Settle, who became apprenticed to the West Yorkshire Garage in 1912. His first job was to clean out a gearbox. "The oil wasn't thin stuff you could run out. It was like butter. You scraped it out with your hands." Some motorists faced the dusty roads wearing goggles. "I didn't. I could never hear as well if I had goggles on."

Tales were told of the rigours of Buckhaw Brow, to the north of the town. "Most of the tales were made up. I personally never had to go backwards." The top of Buckhaw was a popular resting place for motorists, who were inclined to stop and watch fellow motorists struggling up the gradient. In some cases, only the driver would be with the car and his passengers trudged behind. Stopping at the head of the brow was necessary if engines had over-heated during the ascent.

Originally, petrol was sold from cans that were distributed locally by horse and cart. The engine of the Model T Ford, a popular early car, was gravity-fed by fuel from a tank under the seat. At the end of the day, when the level of fuel was low, it was not unusual for the car to jib at a hill because it was suffering from petrol starvation. The headlights operated with acetylene, replenished at the garage from a keg of calcium carbide.

Fred was driving a Model T Ford up Sawley Brow, west of Gisburn, when the engine cut. "On that type of car, the foot-brake was all right but the hand-brake soon wore out. So I was stuck, holding the car with the foot-brake and not being able to get out and replenish the petrol supply." His solution was to grab a jack he carried in the back. With deftness of foot, he slipped from the driving seat and placed the jack under a back wheel before the car could run away. He re-fuelled from a can on level ground – and then walked back to collect the jack!

A distinguished customer at this Settle garage was burly Walter Morrison, who had his "mountain home" at Malham Tarn House and was dubbed the Craven millionaire. He preferred horses to cars but was persuaded to hire a Wolseley car from the Golden Lion Hotel. He had it for a week at a time so he could go off to the Lakes. Then Morrison bought a Fiat and commanded his 75-year-old coachman to collect it from Settle, where Billy Slinger would give him a driving practice. This consisted of being with the coachman for a run round the town while he explained how the car should be driven and, when he lost his patience with his trainee, to simply kick the old chap's foot off the clutch.

The coachman then had to drive the car up the formidable bank from Langcliffe to the stable block at Tarn House which would now become a garage. It is related that when the coachman/chauffeur was approaching the gateway, he shouted *whooa* as usual. The car did not stop, of course. The masonry was struck a glancing blow and the vehicle suffered minor damage. Fred Ellis used to tell me that when the car was driven to the Settle garage for fuel, the corpulent Walter Morrison was usually to be seen sitting across the backseats with his head in a newspaper. As Fred said: "He wouldn't know if he'd stopped or not."

Motorists using the Keighley-Kendal road through Craven in the Twenties began to patronise Barton's garage at Clapham. Founded by Claude Barton, agent of the Ingleborough Estate, it was considered by Thirties motorists to be the best-equipped garage between the West Riding towns and Morecambe. At first, there were two pumps, both hand-manipulated. Cans of aviation spirit and benzole, needed for the sporty cars that drew up in Clapham, were kept just inside the main door in case of fire.

Mr Barton's garagemen attended to the 1918 Austin saloon owned by the Farrers and driven by Teddy Harrison, who regularly drove the family all the way to their London home. Local people gasped when wealthy Mrs Cunliffe took to motoring with such enthusiasm she had her car decorated with cream and black stripes. This meant it was visible at a distance of several miles.

Among the early cars sold at the garage were those named Essex, being comparatively cheap imports from America that achieved world-wide fame as the type of car favoured by Al Capone and his gangsters and featured in many Hollywood films.

Drivers are annoyed when they are impeded, as by a flock of sheep being driven to new pastures. A frustrated driver said to one of the attendants: "Who's the master of this flock?" The answer was an unexpected "that lile black-faced 'un at front."

Skyliners

Charlotte Bronte wrote of a north-country moor as being lonely, silent, still and trackless. This hardly applies today. Once the resort of farmer and gamekeeper, with autumnal visits from grouse shooters, our "vacant, wine-red moors" have lost their sense of desolation. They've been cut about by tracks so the grouse-shooters may be driven to the butts. It is surprising how many people have a legal right of access. Military jets scream as they make low runs over heather and bracken.

Several pubs with moorland settings are called Moorcock after the red grouse, a round-the-year denizen where there is peat and heather. The diet of grouse consists mainly of fibrous heather shoots. Dealing with them needs the grinding action of small pieces of quartz grit, which are taken into the gizzard, plus a specialist gut.

A small-time farmer told me that if I wanted to know what grouse tastes like, I should go to the moor, pull up a piece of heather and chew it. A friend who did not have a grouse moor none the less observed the Glorious Twelfth, opening of the shooting season, by dressing for dinner and sitting down to a meal that included tinned grouse breasts.

The red grouse is a bird to be admired. The moorcock, as a male of the species is known to dalesfolk, is quite a hefty bird, weighing up to one and a-half pounds. The shiny, rufous-brown plumage camouflages a grouse in its skyline habitat of peat and heather. At closer view, you will notice the prominent red eye wattles and a moustachial stripe. The grouse has a considerable vocabulary, greeting a new day from its moorland territory by calling when in flight. The sound is *ka, ka, ka,* beginning with a stutter and then becoming slower. If well done, it proves attractive to any unattached female grouse. Between attracting a mate and defending a territory against rivals, the cock grouse has a busy and stressful start to the spring season. The familiar alarm call the aforementioned *kowa, kowa, kowa,* sounds as though the bird is shouting "go-back, go-back, go-back."

The hen grouse is lighter in colour and takes on a yellowish hue, the plumage being barred, forming an effective camouflage as the bird sits like a feathered tea-cosy on a clutch of eggs among the heather. Grouse chicks are precocious, trying their stubby wings even before they have properly feathered up and taking short flights when you expect them still to be earthbound.

The grouse shooters arrive by four-wheel drive vehicles on tracks surfaced by quarry bottoms. Years ago, they walked to the butts from the nearest roads or, in the case of Jock Yorke and his friends, who had access to moors in upper Nidderdale, from a station on the little single-line track that linked Pateley Bridge with the dalehead. On some moors, the head gamekeeper arranged for local farmers to turn up with their horses to carry the tackle and the food that would be served to the shooters at mid-day.

This, together with wine or spirits, was served in the best of the two rooms of the stone or wood shooting hut at the moor-edge. The other room was for the beaters, who had to be content with beef sandwiches. One year, the beef arrived but the bread was forgotten. The beaters had their sandwiches, trapping a layer of fat between two pieces of lean meat.

Dallowgill Moor, above Nidderdale, is a fascinating tract of 10,000 acres, extending from an elevation of 700 feet to 1,200 feet, which makes it a perfect resort for the red grouse. This is a black [peat and ling] moor; it is hard one for sheep. Winter tends to set in after Christmas and any snow was inclined to lie up there for about a fortnight longer than anywhere else. There were cloudless winter days when the sun is warm on the face and the snow is Daz-white.

Dallowgill Moor is broad and rounded in shape, like a giant hoofmark on the Pennines where the hills begin to dip towards the Yorkshire Plain. Dallow means "dale" and the "gill," a water-carved valley extending up the middle, dividing the moorland into two parts. In the days when the Vyners of Studley presided over Dallowgill, the word of the head gamekeeper was law. If a man fell out with him, the gamekeeper would say to the landlord he thought it was time that the man was leaving. "And that man had to go!"

An average bag of grouse per season was 1,250 brace. The hard-shooting Earl De Grey and Ripon, who dropped dead on the moor after a long day, is commemorated by a special memorial. When the gentry are on the moor, the gamekeeper has to watch his words. One keeper, visiting the local inn at grouse-shooting time, said: "We get all sorts on the moor. I know I've to call a shooter 'sir' and a Duke 'my lord'. Then we got a Bishop. When a grouse got up, I shouted: 'Shoot the little beggar, your holiness' but I could tell by t'expression on his face I was wrong." The tale is (gleefully) told of the new-rich towns-man who wanted some rough shooting. He was not acquainted with sporting etiquette. The visitor was provided with a gun, ammunition and two sporting dogs. He returned shortly afterwards with a request for two more dogs, explaining: "I've already shot the first two."

I last visited Dallowgill in "chancy" weather. Someone turned on a celestial hosepipe. The rain descended on my car roof with a noisy persistency. Tatters of clouds moved aimlessly about the "tops." I heard about "a tight community of people," who for generations had battled against an enemy that was not the king's enemy but the weather.

When Leighton reservoir was being constructed, some men had walks of five or six miles across the moor to work there. If it was rain-ing, they got no work and promptly walked home again.

One of them who awoke to find deep snow across the moor sighed and remarked: "I reckon what we need is a shower o' paraffin – and a flash o' lightning."

In the Picture

Nearly every Dales family has a box or tin full of photographs. In the pre-television age, when "comp'ny" arrived, someone was bound to ask to "look at t'snaps." Everyone – even the kids – chuckled at great grandmother standing by a potted palm in some old-time studio. Uncle Fred had a telegraph pole sticking out of his head. A tiny Selochrome print showed Cousin Ethel on a horse-drawn mowing machine. Today, we're dazzled by images of all kinds ...

An old lady arrived at the studio of the Horner family in Settle, in North Ribblesdale. She was clutching a photograph of her late husband – a faded print of a man wearing a hat. "Will ta do me some copies?" she asked Eddie Horner, adding "wi'out 'is hat." Eddie, who had taken up photography in 1905, said there would be no difficulty but "which side of his head did your husband part his hair?" "Nay, I can't remember," said the customer, "but thou'll see which it is when thou gets 'is hat off."

Eddie's uncle, Michael Horner, who set up the photographic business in 1858, needed a handcart for his tackle when he had an excursion into the district. The camera was bulky – and uncomplicated, for in the absence of a shutter a cap was removed from the lens for the given exposure. Sunlight was almost essential. He also needed a little tent on a tripod as a dark room, for those were the days of "wet plates." They were sensitised, exposed and developed in situ.

In the studio, the background to a photograph was a heavy curtain. The subjects sat or rested their hands on elaborately-carved furniture.

Daylight was the only form of illumination. An exposure of eight or ten seconds was commonplace. For a particularly long exposure – or if there was a restless kid – a metal fork shaped like the letter U was used as a head rest. Only the ends were visible to the cameraman, who touched them out on the negative before making a print. In dry weather, trestle tables were erected in the yard and thirty or forty printing frames placed on them. In each frame was a negative and sensitive paper. The negatives were arranged on the tables in order of density. It took about ten minutes for the image to be transferred to the paper.

A photograph was required of a farmer's child. It was taken on her second birthday. Eddie did his best to amuse her and make her smile. The grave little girl looked up and said: "That's enough." I also heard of the day he photographed a wedding at Keasden. A big feast was laid on in one of the bedrooms, where trestle tables had been set up and all manner of seats brought together for the guests. Eddie's seat was a commode. A relative of the bride, who had clearly had too much to drink, came up to Eddie after the reception and asked him to photograph a pig on a galloway's back.

When Eddie died, there was no one immediately available to take his place. I was cajoled into taking wedding photographs. Week after week, I had the anxiety of checking that the camera contained a film and, looking anxiously at the sky, willing the Weather Clerk to provide "cloudy bright" conditions, neither raining nor too bright, with the sun producing the unwanted "soot and whitewash" effect. Week after week, I returned home from a wedding reception, stuffed with cake and "on edge" in case someone accidentally switched on the main light in my makeshift darkroom.

I had problems galore, such as what to do with the diminutive groom and tall bride (I arranged for the man to stand on a higher step outside the church, which levelled them up) and how to provide proofs that were not so attractive they would be retained by thrifty folk who did not intend to place an order for additional prints. A "happy couple" were hauled away to the reception sitting in a boat (complete with sails) that reposed on a trailer. A relative who arrived too late for a crowd scene was photographed separately and a print deftly fitted in between two others in the group. There were days when the sun was like a blow-torch and another when, at Chapel-le-Dale, mist was so thick I could almost taste it and the bride's once crisp gown and veil hung on her like damp washing.

At my son's wedding reception, two Yorkshire stories I had not heard before were told. The bridegroom said he had a soft spot for his mother-in-law – a bog at the bottom of the garden. A guest told of a dalesman who said that he was sure that his wife had Viking blood. This seemed in accord with early Dales history. Only in this case, the dalesman gave the proof of his statement: "She eats like a norse."

The Kearton brothers, Richard and Cherry, who grew up in Swaledale, took up work in London and as a hobby became photographers. They portrayed the nest of a pair of thrushes in a garden – and, enthused, went to be become pioneer photographers of wildlife. When photographing a pair of nesting merlins, on a tract of moorland, they had a stuffed sheep (recumbent), placed the camera within it and had a long cable release for the shutter. The brother charged with photography concealed himself in a shelter made of peat.

The merlin returned to incubate the eggs. Then a farmer appeared to round up sheep on that part of the moor. He gave whistled commands to his dog and rounded up the sheep in the field – except one, which refused even to get to his feet! No one was more surprised than the farmer when the deception was revealed.

When a photographer visited a Wensleydale farm and asked if he could photograph one of the prize sheep, the farmer brought a splendid specimen to him. The sheep stood for several minutes during the session. Re-visiting the farm two years later, the photographer made a similar request – and was offered the use of what the farmer claimed to be the same prize sheep. "How can you tell one sheep from a hundred others?" queried the photographer. The farmer replied: "I bet you can tell your wife from a hundred women."

John Hey, proprietor of the Silver Star bus company of Carleton, near Skipton, was an old-style photographer who won many a competition, though his technique was scarcely that recommended in text books. As he went through the dark-room procedure of making a print, he had a cigarette clamped between his lips; the rising smoke making him blink. A visitor saw ash drifting down into the developer and noted with surprise how John rubbed parts of the paper with his sleeve to accentuate the development of detail that was underexposed.

Mike Harding carries a camera on his travels through the Dales. Mike, raconteur, broadcaster, writer and photographer of distinction, lives in a house where the windows frame views of Dentdale. My first glimpse of the 200-year-old porched farmhouse came after I had negotiated a rutted track and two blind bends. As a photographer, he shoots in any sort of weather if there is the chance of an unusual effect. One day, visiting Baugh Fell in a roistering, snow-bearing wind, he photographed some inch-thick frost rime on a length of barbed wire. He has photographed Dales farmers, such as Billy Mason of Dale Head Farm, Deepdale, attending to some wool, and "Lal" Billy Lambert of Selside, dosing sheep below Park Fell.

Mike carries a load of photographic gear in a special rucksack that is padded with foam. He used an extreme wide-angle lens at Brigflatts Meeting House so he could remain in the garden and yet include the whole of the building. A ring-flash, used in Hubberholme Church, put a gleam on to one of the carved Thompson mice. He used a powerful telephoto lens – the equivalent of 1,000mm – and a roll and a half of film to get a shot of a crow landing on a tree against a setting sun. The tree was at the head of the dale. He went to the area on three successive evenings to get the desired shot.

Weatherwise

You'd be surprised how many traditional Dales phrases and sayings relate to the weather. Or how clever most farmers are at forecasting. All except one – a grizzle-grey chap, with seamed face and eyes as clear as those of a hawk. I asked him: "What's the weather bahn to do?" He pondered for a long while, then said: "It could do owt."

Bill Foggitt, of Thirsk, a celebrated Yorkshire weather-forecaster, dates his interest to seeing the total eclipse of the sun, on 29 June 1927. The Foggitt family, with a host of other people, planned to see the eclipse from Giggleswick, the most favoured place and the spot where the Astronomer Royal had set up his equipment. A newspaper feature was headed ECLIPSE RUSH TO THE NORTH. Bill remembers it as a crawl rather than a rush. They set off about 4 a.m., the eclipse occurring at 6 a.m. They "crawled" as far as Leyburn Shawl.

"I was very sick and very cold. We got out. We carried pieces of smoked glass. All of a sudden, the moon's shadow passed over the sun. It came in black and cold. The dawn chorus of the birds stopped." At totality, he saw flares, the celebrated corona, coming out of the sun. "I wrote it all down. Father told me to write something every day and I would get a nice diary at Christmas. You didn't get much in your stocking in those days, but sure enough I got a 1928 diary." When I first met Bill he produced that diary for me to scrutinise and commented: "There was a good summer," adding, in a more sorrowful tone, that "King George V was very ill and Thomas Hardy died."

Bill became widely known, to newspaper readers and television viewers, as a weather forecaster with a difference. When I first met him in 1985, and asked him about his forecasting, he distinguished between daily and long-range forecasts. His family's long-time observations on the weather indicated the occurrence of "patterns." The two easiest months to forecast had been April and May. "It's always cold at the beginning of April. Sometimes quite severe. The second part of April is usually warm. It warms up about the 20th. Then you get a setback at the beginning of May." Bill added that the start of April and the start of May coincide with Buchan's two spring cold spells, "each of which lasts about six or seven days."

Bill put much importance on the doings of wild life and plants. Each morning, on rising from his bed at South Villa, a large detached house at the edge of Thirsk, he would scan the barometer. "Locally, you can't beat it for accuracy. It doesn't matter if it's high or low. Is it tending to rise or tending to fall? If I tap it the second time and it's still falling, then I know very well the weather's going to be unsettled." He took note of the wind's speed and direction. In the absence of a weather vane at South Villa, he reached for binoculars and consulted the vane on the church tower at Thirsk.

Bill Foggitt pondered on the appearance of the sky. "If the cloud's dispersing or building up, that's another thing." He recorded the rainfall and looked around for any special natural signs. Midges, for instance. He might notice that midges were "pretty high." A modest man, ever ready to admit any shortcomings, he said he had only recently become aware of the difference between midges and gnats. At the peak of interest, letters flowed in and according to one of them "thousands look to you for guidance." Another letter asked: "How much longer are you going to contribute this slush to the media?" As Bill observed, it does anyone a bit of good now and again to get some criticism. The Sage of Thirsk admired the television forecasters who "keep me on my toes." He had a lucky year in which he got the forecast right and they were wrong. A journalist rang him about the middle of January, when the weather was very severe and asked him how long it was going to last. Bill consulted the barometer, which was falling. He had just noticed that moles were "starting up" and said: "Oh, there'll be a thaw." The journalist asked "when?" Bill thought he would not rush the thaw and he said: "Thursday." That was the day the weather-men brought a new computer into service and forecast a blizzard. Instead, there was a thaw as Bill Foggitt had foretold.

At that time, he went for a three-mile walk almost every day. "When they see me carrying a mackintosh on a sunny day, it makes them think!" One December day he staggered home, chilled to the bone and suffering from hypothermia. He flung himself on a night store heater, then went to bed with a hot water bottle and slept beside it for two hours. "When I woke up, I felt as fit as anything." Typically, on telling me his tale, he added: "The cold spell went on until the second week in January. And the second half of that month was mild."

Despite his strict Methodist upbringing and being a local preacher, Bill's weekday routine included a pint of beer at his local. He practised temperance if not total abstinence. His mind is a repository of worth-while country lore. A journalist working on a brash tabloid newspaper rang him up for some observations about the weather. "I said – 'The cuckoo's silent. That shows it's pretty cold'." Next morning, the headline to the story proclaimed: SILENT CUCKOO TELLS ALL!

Mutton on the Hoof

For centuries, sheep were a mainstay in the Dales. The wool of monastic flocks found a ready and lucrative market on the Continent. Alas, in today's straitened times, the value of a sheep has fallen by some fifty per cent. Some farmers, assessing that the cost of clipping is greater than the price of the fleece, are talking (tongue-in-cheek) of trying to breed a strain of sheep that does not produce wool.

The dale-country reeks of sheep. They are largely responsible for the austere appearance of the fells, for their incessant grazing has prevented the natural regeneration of timber. During and immediately after the last war, gross overstocking of the fells led to the demise of heather over large areas and the spread of an unpalatable grass called *Nardus stricta*.

For our Dales sheep, November is the sexiest time of the year. As another year runs down, with chill winds and a flurry of tinted leaves, the tups on our hill farms attend to their harems of willing ewes. Their prowess is to be seen in the patches of dye on what one farmer calls "t'back end of t'yows." He had smeared dye on the undersides of his selected tups. Some of this dye was transferred to the ewe during the mating act.

If you ever thought of a sheep as being an unromantic creature, then you would have a surprise if you toured the Dales in lustful November, when action is being taken to ensure that another generation of horned sheep will deck the Pennine skyline. The men on the highest farms are in no hurry to release the tups for mating. They do not want lambs to be born at the wildest time of the winter. Now that many farms have big lambing sheds, this is not as important as it was. Farmers, in a spirit of desperation as well as co-operation, have formed a few groups to market their own lambs.

The last thing a Dales flockmaster wants is for tups to injure themselves by fighting over possession of the demure ewes. If, as occasionally happens, two Dales tups are on the same ground when there are ewes about, it's the males who complain of headaches. They back away from each other for a few yards, then charge, meeting skull to skull with a *klonk*, the sound being heard in the next parish. Years ago, when tups began to feel frisky, a farmer might prevent them from fighting each other by attaching a short length of chain from a horn of one to a horn of the other. Whether they liked it or not, they were too close together for combat.

In great grandfather's day, autumn was the time for salving sheep, which was a painstaking and messy job. The salve was a mixture of tar and grease, wi' a lile bit o' milk to tak t'sting out on it. It was once made on the farms, using ingredients bought from dealers. Archangel tar was commonly used in the Dales. Applying the salve was supposed to give the sheep extra protection the winter through; it was also certain death for many sheep parasites like "keds."

The salver sat on the type of stock [seat] used when clipping sheep. A container holding a small quantity of salve was attached to the stock. When a sheep had stopped struggling, its wool was parted lengthways, baring the skin, to which salve was applied by the man, using his forefinger. This parting of the wool was known as "shedding." A second shed was made close by until virtually the whole skin of the sheep had been salved. The job took about an hour. Some men went from farm to farm to help with the salving. They became known as the Black Hand Gang, from the way the tarry mixture worked its way into their skin. It was not unknown for work to continue well into the night, in cramped accommodation and by candlelight. "My grandfadder told me t'air were nearly too thick to breathe," I was told by one old-timer.

There was a curious sequence to salving and that came next spring when, just before clipping of the wool, t'beck was dammed up, creating a pool in which sheep were washed to remove grit and the last traces of salve from the fleeces. As the foul stuff went into the beck, the trout were stupefied and rose gasping to the surface, where they were easily caught. "We used to catch 'em but they weren't worth owt. If tha cooked 'em, they tasted o' tar!"

I had not thought of a sheep as being aggressive towards humans until one day, outside mating time, I walked on a friend's farm. He had allowed me to cross his fields on deer-watching expeditions in some wooded gills. The farmer and I usually chatted in his farmyard before I set off. This day, a faint smile creased his face. I was crossing a large field when I turned to see a sheep making a bee-line for me. There was something about its manner – slightly mad – that made me realise it was not looking to be fed. To a Dales sheep in spring, a ruck-sack means food. Happily, I won the race to the nearest wall. When I returned to the farm, the farmer asked me if I'd met a lively sheep. When I nodded, he said: "I got it cheap at t'auction because it took some handling."

Many Dales sheep are hefted to t'common, which means they drink in a love of the home territory with their mothers' milk and normally do not stray into other areas. The farmer knows where he can find individual animals. This heaf-going instinct, which is also well developed on the Lakeland fells, is worth a lot to the farmer and accounts for the fact that except for a regular change of tup to avoid in-breeding, he is inclined to breed all his own animals.

Indeed, they become part of an extended family. Old sheep and many of the lambs have to be drafted [sold] in order to keep the home flock relatively young and fit. A farmer who has to get rid of his flock, which is a common occurrence in the straitened times today, has to fight to keep back tears as they come under the hammer at the auction mart.

A man whose family has kept horned sheep on the moors for several centuries told me that originally they were just called "crag sheep." Then, with selective breeding, the different strains evolved. Another change was in prospect. His sheep were the Dales-bred sheep to be found in limestone areas of Craven. He was about to change over to Swaledales, which command the best prices because from them can be bred the mule lamb.

As for wool, "which made our wealth, if we had any," it is now worth less than the cost of employing someone to clip the sheep. "Somebody, one day, will breed a woolless sheep," said the farmer with a wink. "Going back a lot o' years, my family kept all the wethers [castrated males] for the wool." He added: "The stocking density is now high. We have drugs and fancy food for sheep, but I haven't noticed that much difference in the death-rate. One sheep is another sheep's enemy."

In these days of form-filling, counting sheep is a serious matter. "My dad counted in three's but I count in two's. When t'Ministry chap comes, we usually count 'em through a gate." I was reminded of an incident in *Ballykissangel*, the popular television series about Irish life, where a local farmer who had been swindling on a grand scale, and who could not find many animals when an official called, heard that it was now possible to count stock by satellite. For days, there was a hammering from an outbuilding. Then, on a never-to-be-forgotten day, the hillside was speckled with painted cut-outs of sheep, providing something for the satellite to fix its high-tech eyes upon.

A remote farm I have enjoyed visiting is Birkdale, at the head of Teesdale. To live there was to be at the mercy of the Pennine weather-gods, especially the god of snow. At Birkdale, the buildings huddle together as though for mutual warmth. No other human dwelling can be seen. Birkdale, though standing at the head of a dale shared by Yorkshire and county Durham, was actually in the parish of Dufton, in Old Westmorland.

A story from the distant past concerns the death of grannie, whose body was strapped to the back of a fell pony, which led a sad procession along the track, beside High Cup Nick and down to Dufton church. The party, arriving early, went into the inn for a warming drink. When they emerged, the pony had slipped its halter and, with the body still strapped to it, had set off for Birkdale. As it approached the farm, excited children – who had been left in the care of an adult – shouted: "Grannie's coming back again!"

I remember Birkdale particularly when it was the home of Brian and Mary Bainbridge, who were at Birkdale for two terms. They arrived for the first time in 1952 with their few possessions stacked on a horse-drawn sled. Flurries of snow filled the area. In those days it seemed to snow at Birkdale for most of the year. Eventually, they had a generator to provide electricity and Calor gas for cooking. They got coal once a year – when they sold their first lot of lambs. "As soon as we have a trailor coming back up empty, we start stocking for the winter."

In 1955, when the growing Bainbridge family experienced its first really grim winter at Birkdale, a hundred gimmer hoggs were lost. The winter conditions in 1963-64 were exceptional. As 1963 drew to a close, snow fell with deceptive gentleness but transformed the familiar contours of the area, leaving heaps to the level of the farm roof. One day in mid-February, the children cheered as a helicopter arrived with the first of several loads of provisions, some food for humans and bales of hay for the farm stock. By spring, it was assessed that some 350 sheep had been lost. It took two years of hard labour, on the farm and, in Brian's case, also working in a local mine, before the family could pay off its debts and rebuild the flock.

They left Birkdale in 1968, after a terrible winter, and returned in 1972. This time their furniture was piled on a tractor-drawn cart which made better progress on the long track from Langdon Beck.

In 1983, snow came out of a clear sky in April. Mary recalled: "It was a lovely day on the Thursday, but by Friday morning we got up to find it was snowing. By dinner-time there was a blizzard and we couldn't see a thing." The sheep, traumatised by the impact of the storm and by some recent injections they had been given, decided to lamb at the same time. "They were dropping lambs in the snow...We put them in the buildings and had a house full of lambs. I was taking milk out of a ewe and feeding any lamb, just to keep it going."

In 1986, snow fell on New Year's Day, then "the winter debated with itself for a bit" and decided to send more snow, which arrived in the second week in January. And so it was – off and on, through the winter, with periods of hard frost laying a crust of ice over the pastures, depriving the sheep of fresh feed. An easterly wind shrivelled up what was left of the herbage and retarded growth. Birkdale Farm was "white over" on 21st May.

> A farmer knocked at the pearly gate,
> His face was scarred and old;
> He stood before the man of fate
> For admission to the fold.
>
> "What have you done?" St Peter asked,
> "To gain admission here?"
> "I've been a farmer, sir," he said,
> "For many and many a year."
> The pearly gate swung open wide
> As St Peter touched the bell.
> "Come in," he said, "and choose your harp –
> "You've had your taste of hell."

Of Dogs and Men

Sheep-farming on the high Pennines grazings would be impossible without a handy way of gathering sheep. This needs to be done in advance of a blizzard or for lambing, dipping, clipping and spaining, the last-named being the separation of yows and their offspring. Help is at hand in the shape of a specially bred and trained dog that has been described as "the Artful Dodger of the Dales skyline." With a name of one-syllable, it worked to the whistle, which is a sort of canine Morse code. Not all dogs respond to training. A favourite cartoon shows a farmer on all-fours, looking towards his sheepdog and saying: "Sitha!"

I have just been introduced to one of the oldest sheepdogs in the Dales. Bess is twenty years old. The North Craven farmer who owns her has no difficult in calculating her age because she was born in the same year as his son. Bess, who was always a useful sheepdog, despite being "a bit short o' size," is now a pensioner. I watched her make a somewhat laboured way across the room. She brushed a chair, sniffed at her master as though for reassurance and settled down to sleep. Having studied this routine, I realised for the first time that Bess was blind.

With an age equivalent to well over a century, in human terms, Bess has a quiet, orderly life. Three years ago, when she "went missing," the farmer thought she had wandered off to die "and we might come across her body in a clump of nettles." Then Bess was seen stumbling along the road to the farm. "We thought she must have had some heart trouble and had laid up till she was better. She's ailed nowt since."

Meanwhile, two other dogs are still on the active staff of the farm. In monetary terms, each is valued at about £2,000 but to the farmer and his family "they're worth their weight in gold." That morning, in lambing time, he and his dog had been out and about at 5-30. It was now one o' clock and, back at home, both were ready for their lunch. The farmer had made a comparatively quick round of the sheep, a matter of fifteen miles across pasture and moorland, thanks to his trusty quad, the four-wheeled mini-vehicle on which he has a comfortable seat. His dog can ride as pillion passenger. In the old days, working on foot, kenning a big flock of sheep would have been a day's job. Did the dog enjoy a ride on the quad? "Aye. Sometimes, it's a job coaxing it off so it can do some work And it's allus ready to jump back again."

One of the family tales, dating back to the 1920s, was of the time grandfather had bronchial trouble and was confined to bed. His trusty dog, anxious about him when he did not appear as usual, sat on the garden wall, looking for signs of its master. Hearing about this, grandfather whistled for the dog, which immediately shot through the open door and up the stairs into the bedroom. This became a daily routine during the three weeks grandfather was bedfast. It was enough for the dog to see its master for a minute or two a day.

When grandfather had been young, he and a dog drove some geese by road for a matter of 12 miles, intending to return home by train. When the train arrived, the lively dog was some distance away and missed catching it. Grandfather embarked, travelled to his home station, then walked the mile or two home. The dog, which must have followed the train, was already there to greet him.

Sam Dyson, who farmed in the Bronte Country, was well-known throughout the Dales as a judge at sheepdog trials. One of the first dogs he bought on taking up farming was "a little hairy dog. It had a bit of a beard. It cost me five pounds. When I was about to take it home, the chap who sold it to me said: 'Whatever you do, don't let it off t'lead for a week or two or it'll come straight back home. We've sold it afore and it allus comes back'."

Sam's wife, Peggy, rubbed the dog's feet with butter and when it had licked the butter off she pronounced the dog would not run away. "It never went nowhere, 'cept where it should. The fields were full o' sheep, as usual, and that dog ran those sheep. Wherever they went, it was just there in front of 'em. If they went through a gap 'oil or over a wall, it was waiting for 'em. It was a marvellous dog."

Sam developed his own way of training a dog – of how to respond to those shrill, unemotional, uncomplicated whistles that signify "go left," "go right," "go back a bit," "come in a bit" and so on. I said: "You make it sound easy." Sam replied: "It depends how good t'dog is. Some picks it up like nowt. Some's hard work." He brushed away my point that working two dogs simultaneously was difficult. "I've seven dogs nah; they're not on t'same whistle." He demonstrated the point by whistling towards his terrier, which had been asleep, doubtless chasing rabbits across the broad fields of its mind. The terrier leapt up and almost tore itself in two.

Peggy said that when she persuaded Sam to go shopping with her, and they'd spent what he thought was enough time in the super-market, he never went looking for her. He whistled. When Peggy told a friend about this, she said: "He wouldn't whistle at me, you know." Peggy replied that he would if he'd lived with her for fifty years. In a crush, Peggy is guided by Sam who resorts to the "left" and "right" commands.

Sam judged at Northallerton. Two brothers were among the com-petitors. One was a champion ploughman. "He put his dog off and they picked these three sheep up. They were big, heavy sheep. It browt 'em through t'first obstacle. As they were coming through, one sheep laid down. So he left that and went on. He started on his drive away and got to the hurdle. Another sheep dropped on t'floor. So I thought: 'It's no good going on judging any longer'. But he still went on. He got to t'pen. There was only one sheep left. When the stewards checked up, they found two dead sheep. I bet there's no other man in England has lost two sheep and tried to pen the other."

In his later years, Sam's memories of dogs were prompted by look-ing at photographs of them. There was Tim. "I could tell that dog to sing – and it'd sing!" Another photograph: "That was Lad. I selled it to Leet Harry [Huddleston]." There being two Harry Huddlestons, one was known as Leet Harry and the other as Dark Harry. Asked about sheepdogs, he would reply: "I've had some good 'uns and I've shot a few." Sam said you wanted a dog with "a bit o'class and enough eye to steady itself on the job. You don't want a dog that is forever flying about."

Size didn't matter to Sam. "Good 'uns don't come oft enough. Today you see lots of nursery dogs do a lot of trialling; then you never see them no more. They've fallen to bits with overwork." The best type of dog was one that would stand straightening-up [training] and yet remain pals with its owner. "If it starts to sulk or owt like that, you don't get nowhere. Start praising a dog for doing wrong – and it's no good at all. When you've told it off and you're ready to forgive it, yon dog should be ready to forgive you."

He observed: "Many of the trials dogs have been bred and trained for that job. They're not worth thruppence on t'moor. They'd get lost in two or three minutes." He added: "Sometimes, with t'wind reight, you're working a dog up to three-quarters of a mile away."

In the Wet

For the guidebook writer, the Dales are always sunlit. Like the bees, a guidebook photographer operates only in sunny conditions. To Heaton Cooper, the Lakeland artist, there were no such things as good and bad days. They were either dry or wet. He could enjoy any climatic condition. It was distinctly wet when Bob and I went for a walk in limestone country. It was to be more interesting than enjoyable.

In one of the early issues of *The Dalesman* appeared an article entitled "It always rains in the Dales." Outrage! Letter after letter recalled balmy, sunlit days. The author of the article, tongue in cheek, wrote "It never rains in the Dales." I thought of him as I glanced across a murky North Ribblesdale. Not even the limestone scars, which are normally so cheerful, could raise a smile.

The weather forecast was for sunshine with showers, some of which might be heavy. We spent hours in teeming, tippling, pattering, gurgling precipitation. Conditions improved only in the last half mile of the walk. Then, as Bob said, memorably: "It's got less worse."

We set off at a time when the Weather Clerk had turned off the hosepipe, though the trees were dripping from a recent storm. Bob fancied himself as a botanist. As we admired loosestrife and rosebay willow-herb, the rain descended and we cocooned ourselves in waterproof clothing.

We strode squelchingly along the Stackhouse road. Bob identified yet more wayside plants – pink campion, giant bellflower, meadow cranesbill. A little owl – small, wide-eyed, with a flattened head giving it a comical appearance – was perched on the gable end of a disused building just beyond the hamlet. It moved its head jerkily from side to side, as though trying to keep us in focus. Then it flew briskly across a field and found a new perch on one of the capstones of a drystone wall.

Yellow lines had been painted beside the road at the approach to Knight Stainforth. A red telephone kiosk had been placed near the caravan site. We descended to Stainforth Bridge, which spans the Ribble like a petrified rainbow. Water cascaded from every leaf on a row of trees. Raindrops bounced off the butterbur's green umbrella.

We had what Bob called a butty-stop while standing beside a wall under a leaking tree. Beside the wall grew some fine specimens of red dead-nettle. Bob invited me to grasp it. I preferred to grasp a pork pie, even though the rain was rapidly diluting the gravy. The river, stirred by the downpour, was the colour of pale ale. George, an old friend of mine, made a speciality of describing views in relation to various drinks. He would probably have likened the river water to whisky.

Across the river, a steep hillside was a riot of floral colour, which would have looked well on a photograph – if I had brought a water-proof camera. There was betony galore, said Bob. Puddles were now classifiable as tarns. The drumming of rain on my anorak hood was beginning to make me feel sleepy.

We trudged up the lane to a bridge spanning the Settle-Carlisle line. The embankments were ablaze with rosebay willow-herb which, said Bob, is also known as fireweed. Railway photographers converge on Dent station when the embankments are aglow with the plant. A Sprinter train in the modern livery of green, streaked with yellow, made little sound as it ran over a length of spanking new rail. I preferred the old type with the familiar clickety-clack produced by wheels crossing rail joints.

At Stainforth, we found sanctuary in a telephone kiosk, not to ring for an update on the weather forecast, or for the lifeboat, but to consult the map before it became pulp from exposure to the elements. Crucially, we wanted to find the start of the path to Winskill in a part of the village where building was taking place. Soon we were slithering on wet grass and glistening limestone. The path became a narrow stairway in woodland as dense and dripping as a jungle. My spectacles steamed up. Booted feet slithered on rock filmed by water.

We emerged in the meadows of Low Winskill which are cared for by the landowner to the extent of being kept clear of artificial fertilisers, which elsewhere have decimated the field flora. There's nowt like "muck" for reviving jaded meadowland in the Dales. Bob intoned the names of some of the plants as though in a litany: Ladies bedstraw, knapweed, harebell, betony galore, tormentil, eyebright…

The weather seemed to ease. Or were we past caring? We passed Low Winskill and gained the metalled track that led us near Sampson's Toe (an erratic, resting on limestone) to the Langcliffe road and on, by green path, in mist and renewed rain, to a new kissing-gate giving access to the area where a limestone cliff appears to be yawning. A product of over-enthusiastic nineteenth century archaeology, the vast hole is known as Victoria Cave.

Here there was not even a jackdaw to greet us. Driven into one of the Victorian slagheaps, now grassed over, was a signpost giving details of the place over a span of 120,000 years, when the cave filled with layers of clay as glaciers melted and re-thawed annually. Locked up in the clay were the remains of ancient beasts. We occupied the latest layer, composed partly of litter.

As I sat munching tomato sandwiches in the wet (ugh!) I reflected on a winter day of 1991 when it was snowing, not raining. Arriving at the Cave in a white-out, we found it adorned with icicles and watched the wind play games with drifts of powdery snow. Today, there was murk, greyness, rain and yet more rain, to which we must return. We followed the cragside path as gruff voices heralded the approach of two ravens, which were black playthings of the wind.

With the rain intensifying, we took the direct route to Settle, descending the Banks with an awareness that the western sky was brightening. We saw a patch of blue, "big enough to patch a Dutchman's trousers," as the old dalesfolk said when they were looking for signs of good weather in haytime.

PS – Bob rang me later to claim an extra three miles of walking. He had gone back to look for a missing walking stick.

A Day at Muker

I have been reflecting on a Muker Show of the late 1980s – though such is the element of tradition in Swaledale great changes are not likely to occur. T'show is for dalesfolk. Visitors are welcome – so long as they dean't git in t'way. Ewes suffer a total loss of dignity when they are turned on their backs, then reared into a sitting position, where their bellies sag. As a farmer explained: "T'judges want to know if tits are reight. Some tits can be duds."

As I reached the entrance to the field, the steward advanced on me with a broad smile and outstretched hand. I expected a handclasp. Instead I received a blow from a rubber stamp. The steward relieved me of £1 and I entered the showfield. On my hand, in purple capitals, was stamped the name MUKER, proof that I had paid for admission.

A farmer said: "Thoo wants to be thankful we didn't use a hornburn or clip a bit out of an ear." That's the way they had dealt with sheep since Norse times.

It had been a wild night, with spiteful showers. Now the clouds were parting to admit the radiance of golden September sunshine. The tents were shaking themselves dry. A score of bandsmen and bandswomen, members and friends of Muker Silver Band, formed a circle near *The Farmers' Arms*. When I mentioned "Silver" to a local man, he replied: "We're a bit more posh than a brass band." The bandsmen did look smart in their uniforms of burgundy and black with silver embellishments.

The band rendered that lively tune *Slaidburn,* named after the Bowland village, and when a few more tunes had been played, three show officials formed a line and the band fell in behind. They marched with that distinctive short-stepped bandsman's gait that is purposeful without over-taxing t'old uns.

In a quiet corner of the showfield, the finest Swaledale tups (here known as *tee-ups*) stood with haughty looks on their dark faces and with horns looking like drop handlebars. Black face and grey muzzle mark out the "Swardle" breed of sheep which will be seen on the emblem of the Dales National Park , until some bright-spark alters it, and was also on a signpost at *The Farmers' Arms.*

The farmers were too busy for much conversation. I watched a man attaching labels to tufts of wool on the backs of his sheep. "Do the labels stay on?" I asked. A minute or two passed and he replied, simply: "Some on 'em do." A man who was "fluffing up" wool on the fleece of a sheep – wool that had doubtless been crushed as the animal was in transit – explained this titivating operation as being "like what a woman does afore she goes out anywhere. She wants to look pretty."

If the judges were awestruck at the presence of some of the keenest breeders of sheep in the hill country, they did not show it. A young judge had already developed the art of dallying so that he kept everyone in suspense. The judges took in the general characteristics of the sheep and then moved closer, parting the wool, testing its quality and looking for "black bits."

The sheep were released, while being kept in a limited area as the judges studied each animal's carriage. Then the owners recaptured them, collectively, advancing side by side with arms outspread, jamming the sheep in a corner and then grabbing the down-curved horns. Nature might have had hill farmers in mind when the ponderous horns were developed.

As they deliberated, the judges looked appropriately grave. This was a serious matter. They peered at the sheep, made the occasional sortie to check on some minor detail and then considered which animals would be awarded the prize tickets. A few minutes ticked by. The red, blue and yellow rosettes – representing first, second and third places – were distributed and Muker Show had a set of superstars at which farmfolk might gawk with admiration for the rest of the day.

I asked a farmer if he agreed with the judges. He thought a minute, then said: "They're not far oot."

One of the speakers at the lunch that provided a satisfying interlude in the varied events of the day referred to the Dales as a "cared-for landscape which did not just happen." The tradition of Swaledale, he added, lay in the hand and heart and efforts of the farming community.

I returned to the sheep pens. A latecomer arrived. "Hoo is ta?" asked one man, to be told: "All is safely gathered in. Taties oot. Cows laid in." They don't believe in wasting words in the Yorkshire Dales.

A Postman's Life

We tend to take our postmen (and women) for granted. They are the most local, friendly and reliable aspect of officialdom. Postman Pat, the creation of John Cunliffe, was devised as a dalesman. He operated from the fictitious hamlet of Greendale with inspiration drawn from Longsleddale, in Old Westmorland. This cheery little postman with Jess, a black and white cat, raised the profile of the rural postman and also introduced hosts of children to subsidiary characters, including Mrs Goggins, Ted Glen, the Rev Timms and Peter Fogg.

John Cunliffe got to know Longsleddale when he was a student teacher engaged in teaching practice at nearby Selside. When I asked him about his creation, he said that it was partly inspired by a film he had seen of the work of a country postman who, unlike many of his city colleages, did rather more than collect and deliver mail. He performed lots of jobs for country folk, such as collecting medical prescriptions.

The red vans of the Post Office are a familiar sight throughout the Dales. Yet when I began my Dales wanderings, most of the rural postmen travelled on foot or by bike. They did so cheerfully, as though they really enjoyed their work. The vanborne postman who has remote farms on his rounds still has an athletic life, opening and closing gates that divide the big fields.

Tommy Brown, of Gunnerside, delivered letters to 45 lonely farms in Swaledale in all weathers for 45 years. It took him six hours to cover a round of from 12 to 15 miles. Jack Rukin, of Keld, included Tan Hill Inn on his round. He was the only regular contact the residents had with the outside world.

Fred Falshaw, a postman in Upper Wharfedale, told me that at one point he had to ford the river. If there was a spate, he would attach any mail to a stone and hurl it across. One day, he reached the river bank to find the farmer waiting for him on the other side of the water. He attached a postcard to a stone. The stone landed at the feet of the farmer but the postcard, becoming detached, fell into the river and was swept away. Said the farmer: "Nivver mind, Fred. Tell me what were on't."

"Postie" could not dodge the home of the Browns at Cosh, one and a-half miles beyond the head of Littondale. Mrs Brown, anxious to have some fresh topics of conversation, ordered a daily newspaper by post. She thus ensured a regular visit from the postman.

The Newall family recorded long years of service to the Post Office at Bolton Abbey. Roy Newall retired in 1958 after 40 years on the Storiths round. He recalled when King George V was a notable guest of the Duke of Devonshire during the grouse-shooting season. The king arrived with a large retinue of servants. His mail was delivered to the back door of the big house, where it was received by a footman who handed it to the butler. This worthy handed it to the king. The postman was given a glass of beer.

The Dales postman assumed heroic proportions in times of heavy snow, notably during the late winter and early spring of 1947. On Malham Moor, the postmen took turns, day after day, to walk the four miles from Langcliffe to the farmsteads. Edith Carr recalls that the mail was frequently left at her home, Capon Hall, to await collection by neighbouring farmers. When a postman entered the kitchen in the early afternoon, he was a sorry sight, his outer clothes stiff with the cold and his eyebrows and hair covered with rime.

Mr Chaffers, short and stout, was determined that thick snow would not stop His Majesty's mail from getting through. He arrived at the farm with great ceremony, puffing and blowing. He would then unpeel his waterproof leggings and the brown paper and newspaper he had wrapped round his legs, securing the wrappings with thick, coarse string.

He had great faith in his "thermal" wear and he trundled for miles, looking for all the world like a well-wrapped parcel.

In the Pulpit

For many years, the strength of Dales Methodism lay in its small army of local preachers – cheerful volunteers who addressed friends and relatives with easy informality. Not all of them had passed examinations. They were known as auxiliaries. It was the beginning of the end for a host of rural chapels when the auxiliaries were given the option by Conference of formally qualifying or ceasing to be "on the Plan."

Local preachers who had been born and reared on the hill farms of the Yorkshire Dales preached from the heart, not the head. The only book-larning most of them did was to regularly read the Bible and *Farmer's Weekly*. They had graduated from the University of Life.

Sermons were prepared late at night while sitting at the deal table in the kitchen and by the light of a paraffin lamp. Salted pig meat hung from hooks in the ceiling. The oatcake that had been put on a rack to dry looked for all the world like wash-leathers.

One of the most enthralling sequences in a short series of television programmes about Yorkshire farming in crisis was filmed for Channel 4 in the lile chapel at Farndale, on the North York Moors. The chapel and chapelgoers were not unlike those at a host of places of worship in the western dales.

A local preacher, one of many who had come on hard times and were now classed as "a dying breed" announced the theme of his address at a Harvest Thanksgiving service. He produced from a bag what he had described as a visual aid. It was a monster specimen from a root crop grown as animal feed. In a short, simple address – a modern Parable – to a fretful rural congregation, he said if his listeners wanted a title, it was – don't give up.

Farmers, he added, were a misunderstood people. The majority of politicians and general public were unaware of the current crisis. Having drawn the monstrous root from his bag, he added that this was evidence of a crop "where we nearly gave up." Not all were of this size; there were many that were smaller and a few that were larger. "You never know, do you, friends?" In his slow measured speech he added: "Once they started to grow – and there's a spiritual parallel here – we kept scrufflin' 'em. And you know that when you scruffle something, it stirs the plant. And sometimes we have to be stirred to grow. That is why we should never give up."

Long after the worshippers had forgotten the fine points of that address, or the sale of the harvest produce that had been neatly arrayed for the Harvest service the previous day, they would remember the words of the farmer-preacher.

My old Grannie, aged ninety-four, classified one man who had occupied the pulpit of her chapel as "a teacher – not a preacher." In a brilliant academic career he had collected half a dozen degrees. Most of what he said would have impressed fellow academics but was unintelligible to his congregation.

Many tales are told of local preachers, the most notable being when a Member of the Flock said: "I had a locust preacher to tea t'other Sunday." Her friend corrected her. "It's local, not locust preacher. A locust settles in a place and eats all afore it." The first speaker said: "Aye – that's what this chap did."

Anglican parsons tended to be somewhat dry and services more cut-and-dried than those favoured by Nonconformists, one of whom rebuked a new preacher for reading his prayers. He added: "Prayers should come from thee heart, not a sheet o' paper." There was a steward who, just before a service, asked me (the preacher) if I was nervous. I nodded. "Nay, lad," he said, "we should be more frightened o' thee than thou is of us."

Jolly Jack

When you are not stained glass window-gazing in Hubberholme church, at the head of Wharfedale, look for the plaque commemorating J B Priestley, author and playwright. His ashes lie in the churchyard. He had first visited the place during a walking tour in 1919. It was a time of healing after the mental ravages caused by Army service during the First World War.

JB was conscious of his image, which was almost Churchillian, except that whereas the politician smoked a cigar Priestley's fancy was a pipe, from which – at times of intense work – smoke poured as though from a mill chimney when there was a rush order for cloth. The two men were noted for the originality of their ideas. Neither had ever resorted to clique. He said in later life: "I am more a writer than I am a human being."

Priestley, a literary lion of the inter-war years and a broadcaster with something of the Churchill spirit during the 1939-45 war, spent most of his life "down South." He retained vivid memories of pre-1914 Bradford – or Bratford, as the locals call their city. His Yorkshireness was perpetuated, in the alien atmosphere of the South Country, by a blunt, forthright nature, such as one might find in the old West Riding in which his childhood and adolescence were spent. He considered the Hubberholme area to be one of the fairest on earth.

Here you find the old church and a bridge over the Wharfe. It is related that after a particularly wet spell, when the river overflowed, fish were found swimming between the pews. On the opposite bank of the river is a pub, the *George Inn*, which attained an additional measure of fame when the doors of the outside toilets were labelled "tups" and "yows". JB was fond of visiting the inn, observing that if he was younger he would have enjoyed being the landlord of the place.

A photograph shows him trudging along the track behind Hubberholme church. We see only a back view of JB but there is enough for an interested person to be able to identify him. You noticed that dark beret, with a fringe of coarse grey hairs, the chubby body covered by a well-worn raincoat, those heavy shoes and the pipe, smoke billowing, joining the cumulus clouds above the dale.

JB's immediate post-war visit to the Dales was paid for by the Editor of *The Yorkshire Observer*, who had been persuaded to give him a guinea a time for a short series of articles on a walking tour. He set off through a sunlit landscape, with dew sparkling like diamonds in the meadows. He was unbelievably happy. I never thought of JB as he might have been in a happy frame of mind. On the occasions I met him, he was somewhat gruff. Someone wrote of him that he had so many chips on his shoulders there'd be enough to start a fire.

He grumbled about Dales weather, which was inclined, during his visits, to be wet and windy – not the sort of conditions he would have preferred as as an amateur artist whose favourite medium was gouache. Like many another painter, he found the transient nature of our Pennine lighting effects very frustrating. JB grumbled about Dales food, which he considered was better years ago. "There were not the caterer's tricks. The food was simpler, with less attempt to make a hotel meal out of it." One of these caterer's tricks was with regard to pies. "It is the essence of a pie, whether a meat pie or a fruit pie, that the crust is baked with the pie and is part of it." Nowadays, there was a tendency to stew some fruit or meat and add a square of crust done separately. "This is not a pie. It irritates me when I encounter it." (I had not met such a "trick" in the Dales, where the native apple pie is unchanged).

JB could tell a pithy Yorkshire tale, such as that of the daleswoman who in the 1930s had visited Kettlewell once a week to shop and then broke with custom. A friend asked her why. She said: "I can't stand t'racket." Dorothy, wife of Harry Scott, the founder of *The Dalesman*, was fond of recalling a story which JB told against himself. When *The Good Companions*, a work that established him as a celebrity, was first staged at the Grand Theatre in Leeds, he was keen to know what the average theatregoer thought about it. He mingled with the dispersing crowd, listening for comments. An elderly couple came out. The man looked glum. He said to his wife: "Well, thou would cum."

Wensleydale was his favourite dale. He regarded it "as a sort of anchorman to the whole thing." He thought the Dales villages had changed less than in any other part of England he knew, with the possible exception of a small section of the Cotswolds, which had been carefully planned and controlled. Bainbridge, where he stayed, looked very little different from what it did forty years ago.

The last time I saw him, he was with Jacquetta, his wife, at Muker in Swaledale. He loved the dalehead villages. He was seventy years of age. Behind him was an enormous outpit of words. His travels had taken him to many parts of the world, and not long before he and Jacquetta had been in Red China. Yet he could return to the Dales with the old sense of wonder and delight. As he had written in the first issue of *The Dalesman* way back in 1939: "The Dales never disappoint me." To him, the dalesfolk, when talking among themselves, sounded Scandinavian, rather like minor Ibsen characters. He added: "But they are good people, not yet corrupted by tourism."

The great man died in 1984 after a short illness. He was cremated. His ashes reposed under the staircase of a local farmhouse for a week before the committal service took place, which was on a wild and chilly spring day when the farmers were busily engaged with lambing-time and the attendance was not as large as one might have expected. He lives on through the words he spun and pictures taken of him, such as a televised record of a meeting with his son, Tom, not long before JB died.

We saw JB lean back in his chair, relaxed and contented. We watched him strike a match. Was ever a match struck with more telling effect? We waited for the smoke to clear, for the bowl of the briar to glow, for JB to talk about his early life in Bradford. A photograph of an old bearded man was passed to him with a request for identification. "It's my grandfather," said JB. He pondered on the picture of a man with a grizzle-grey beard and added, in typical Priestley fashion: "He looks like everybody's grandfather."

Back to Nature

True naturalists are, by the very nature of their interest, solitary, somewhat odd people. They keep unsociable hours, skulk behind beards, habitually use Latin names for birds, beasts, blooms and bugs and spend hours squinting through binoculars, telescopes or microscopes. Of the Dales naturalists I knew, Bill Shuttleworth ringed swallows, Chris Cheetham had a species of daddy-longlegs named after him and Keith Briggs listened in to conversations between adders and whistling deer.

Fred, one of my companions on jaunts into the north-country, was interested in wildlife only from the point of view of what was edible. He usually tasted grouse on the Glorious Twelfth. On a visit to Scotland, he had consumed a capercaillie sandwich.

Fred's favourite story was about owls, which of course are inedible – except perhaps to another owl. A townsman and a countryman were out walking when the twilight shivered to a blood-curdling scream. "What was that?" asked the alarmed townsman. The countryman said it was an owl. "I know that," said the townie, "but what was 'owling?"

A former vicar of Giggleswick who was a keen taxidermist and also a fine cook sometimes let his stomach rule his mind. When a dead bird was brought to him to be "stuffed," he might debate with himself whether to preserve it – or eat it.

When I first commuted over Buckhaw Brow, between my home at Giggleswick and *The Dalesman* office at Clapham, black rabbits gavorted on the grassy area leading up to the limestone scars. Later, I came under the unblinking stare of a family of owls. These were the so-called little owls, which are not only small but have flattened heads, giving them a comical appearance – and also, I suspect, deterring anyone who, like Fred, might associate them with a cooking pot.

A pair of owls had "squatted" in one of the rabbit burrows. In due course, I saw young owls standing gravely at the entrance to the burrow, waiting for their parents to return with food. I mentioned the owls to Bill Shuttleworth, a farmer friend who was an authorised ringer of birds, placing light alloy rings on the legs of nestlings so that a check might be kept on their travels.

Bill duly arrived. To him, an owl in the hand was worth two in the burrow. I thought we ought to get permission from the landowner. Bill brushed this idea aside. Everyone knew Bill and his work of ringing birds, he said. Unhappily, the next people to appear were a brace of policemen, new to the idea. Bill muttered something about having to milk and returned to his farm. I did my best to explain our intentions. One of the (kindly) policemen rang me up later, gave me the name and telephone number of the landowner and suggested I might give him a ring about "owling."

It was one of Bill's "ringing" friends who invited me to go "swifting." He explained that he intended to visit a former barn where swifts nested under the eaves. It was a warm, calm evening and swifts uttered piercing screams as they skated across the sky. The barn stood near the centre of a small town and was being used as a garage by several local men. The bird-ringer propped a ladder against the barn, clambered up with a crowbar and began to prise up stone roof-flags to enable him to reach for the young birds in their nests.

A lady who had been watching him from a house just across the street said he had been "swifting" at her home the previous year "and ivver since it's rained in." I made myself as inconspicuous as possible. Mercifully, the operation did not take long. I heard later that the swift-ringer had been to a dance with his wife that evening, taking with him several of the parasites that infest swift nests and live off the blood of swiftlets. His dancing was particularly erratic as the lice made their presence felt on various parts of his body.

Stan Lythe, of Grassington, had enough patience to locate the ground nest of a pair of short-eared owls, which dalesfolk knew as moss owls. He had official permission to place a hide near the nest so he might photograph them. Early that springtime we had watched a short-eared owl circling on its long wings, which it suddenly brought together, beneath its body, several times – producing a sound like clapping. He then located the lekking place of black grouse (a bird which in recent years has dwindled until few remain in the dale-country). A blackcock, the male of the species, is a big bird – as big, to quote a gamekeeper, "as a littleish turkey." Stan, wandering across "white" moor in autumn found a lek, where the pounding feet of grouse had produce a circle where the vegetation was crushed until it resembled coconut matting.

At this display area, cock birds gather, facing up to each other in pairs to prance and display and make strange sounds, including a pigeon-like cooing and a popping sound like a cork being taken from the neck of a bottle. Visiting females, which are known as greyhens, tend to want to be mated by the strongest birds – those that have the central part of the lek, hence the anxiety to be there.

In good time for the spring display, Stan raised a hide beside the lek and here we gathered, an hour before the birds were due to arrive. Their appearance was dramatic. They came from different directions but, to the dictates of a diurnal clock, touched down at about the same time. It was April and rather than get up long before dawn to be at the hide by first light, I elected to go in the late afternoon. Stan had placed his hide so well that one of the large blue-black birds, walking with inflated wattles, drooping wings and white under-tail feathers that showed up brightly, tried to force a way between the hide and a guy rope.

Chris Cheetham, who died many moons ago, was one of the last of the Victorian naturalists – a man from a well-off textile family who quit his milltown job for Austwick, where he no longer felt the need to shave nor, indeed, to be well dressed. He wore shorts for most of the year. Chris had two cycles – a normal one and a tandem, on which he took his ninety year old mother for "spins." He was an expert botanist but delighted in the mini-world of insects. Incorporated in the Latin name of a species of daddy-long legs was the word *Cheethami*.

As a naturalist, Derek Bunn was most fond of dusk, or what the old dalesfolk called "t'edge o' dark." For years, he studied barn owls in a semi-forested area at the head of the Hodder valley. His main hiding tent was set up beside a plantation and overlooked a glade in which stood an outbarn. The owls were entering it through an old forking-hole at the gable end during a long nesting season. Sometimes, when he had another appointment, I occupied the hide and kept notes on the birds' behaviour.

I must reach the hide without disturbing the owls. A disturbed barn owl has a series of ringing calls. Happily, I never triggered off the alarm because I approached the hide on hands and knees through an unbrashed part of a conifer forest where branches threatened to rip the shirt off my back. One summer evening, clouds of midges danced in beams of sunlight as the owlets stimulated their parents to go food-hunting by uttering "snoring" calls that rose to fever pitch in antici-pation of a feast. I would then see a parent owl winging silently through the glade like a big white moth, except that this "moth" had a vole dangling from one of its talons.

Soon, the youngsters began to appear, looking shining white in their new plumage. When the youngsters first flew, they alighted on the roof of the hide I was occupying. Looking up, I saw their claws showing through the hessian a foot or so above my head.

Keith Briggs, a first-rate field naturalist living in Barnoldswick, first thought he would take up bird photography and then decided to invest in sound-recording equipment. He would record the songs and calls of birds and beasts. Part of his equipment was a large reflector, which he usually carried at shoulder height. Early one morning, he emerged from a grove of rhododendrons as a man was walking by. The man turned and fled, doubtless thinking he had encountered a Man from Mars.

Any natural sounds came within the orbit of his interest. He had a miscellany of hisses from a colony of adders, one of which ate two eggs laid by a nightjar. He found that thrushes in Upper Wharfedale were absorbing in their songs phrases from the repertoire of green woodpecker and nuthatch. Another thrush used the titter of a spar-row hawk.

As I was engaged in a long-term field study of sika deer in Bowland, I introduced Keith to a local farmer whose home meadow was being frequented by a stag with its hinds during the autumnal rut. Keith saw an excellent opportunity of recording the high-pitched sika squeals, which sound like clear whistles when heard distantly. He set up his equipment at dusk. Unfortunately, the farmer and his family were away visiting friends. They had been delayed. The cows were bawling to be milked.

The farmer said Keith might return any time and, this being Keith, he was back in the early hours. One of the farmer's daughters awoke to hear the car approaching and saw a shadowy figure near the house. She alarted dad, who rang the police, who sent a constable in a car to investigate. It so happened that the constable was based in Barnoldswick and immediately recognised Keith. The incident ended with coffee in the farm kitchen and Keith's promise to return at a more sociable time.

Mr Farrer's Rhodies

Reginald Farrer, who is revered by gardeners, especially those who cultivate rock plants, was born in London but raised at the family home, Ingleborough Hall, at Clapham, where he established a natural rock garden on the cliff above Ingleborough Lake, firing seeds to unhandy places, using a mussel-loading gun. His chief rock garden was in the grounds of the hall. Charles Graham, a disciple of Farrer, revived one of his great schemes.

The driveway through Clapham Woods, which is open to the public on payment of a modest charge, traverses an area where, in spring, the woodland floor is a mass of bluebells, dog's mercury and anemones. The dark waters of Ingleborough Lake are retained by an earthen dam. At the head of the lake, Fell Beck has carved for itself a gorge that, with groves of rhododendrons and bamboos, resembles a Himalayan valley. In an area which is generally of limestone, Farrer adorned the sides of the gorge with plants he had collected in the Far East. A springtime spectacle is created by the bright blossoms of the rhodies, which give the woods a carnival atmosphere.

Farrer's short life of forty years was in every way unusual. He was born with a hare-lip, which he eventually covered with a bushy moustache. A bachelor, who loved solitude, his approach to plant life was both scientific and emotional. He became a Buddhist and dressed accordingly when giving a lecture about his travels, his voice being somewhat squeaky. He dedicated a book to one of his Siamese cats. Visiting Mr Redhead's garden near Bolton-by-Bowland he prostrated himself before a shrub for which he had a special regard.

Farrer sought plants in the alpine areas of Europe and the Far East and introduced many species to English gardens. An impulsive man, he once set off for Clapham railway station, a mile and a-half from the village, with carpet slippers on his feet. He booked a seat for London, then contacted his family and asked them to send on the money and equipment he would need for yet another overseas jaunt.

What Farrer had planted in his short but busy life was, in the 1970s, in need of rejuvenation. The rhododendrons were suffering from over thirty years of neglect. Enter Charles Graham, who had retired to Giggleswick after forty years spent in industrial management. Charles, a long-time plant enthusiast and a devotee of the work of Farrer, voluntarily did the work. He went forth with saw, axe and garden fork, a "committee of one."

He kept unsociable hours. Joan, wife of Dr J A Farrer, owner of the estate, recalls that he was an "early bird" and arrived in the village at about 6 a.m., driving an ancient blue car that only he was able to control. He sauntered into the woods carrying a mass of assorted objects, from string to spade, and in due course, had a snack meal of cheese and dry bread. By 2-30, he was returning home, here to dine on boiled onions before slipping into bed for a couple of hours to rest and read. A friend said he had "a thirsty mind."

At first, he felled any unwanted sycamore, hazel and birch. Tarzan-like he used a rope to swing along the sides of the gorge with saw and axe, clinging to the part he wished to clean up and from which unwanted trees would be removed. He then descended to beck level to remove a tangle of fallen wood. He found seedlings that had lodged in moss or between tree roots. Some were even struggling in crannies in the outcropping slate. They were transported from Clapham to his home at Giggleswick – a house situated on a thinly wooded hillside – where they were given nursery conditions until he judged it wise to return them to the wild.

Charles would proudly show me his little nursery plot beside the house, glibly reciting the scientific names of the plants. The seedlings grown in pans were transferred into peat beds. In 1983, some of his reintroduced plants were four feet high and in flower.

When, during his woodland work in winter, a tree rolled on him, he walked back to the village using the shaft of his fork as a crutch. He was laid up at home for six weeks and passed the time naming plant paintings that Reginald Farrer made on his expeditions to the Far East. He classified species of rhododendron from a collection of transparencies. Charles died in 1986, at the age of 87. Not long before, I had accompanied him to the area of dark grey rock above Ingleborough Lake where he showed me evidence of his work. He did not brag. He simply and quietly related what had happened.

A monument to Farrer – minus the angel that originally surmounted it – is to be seen in a memorial garden just off the terrace at Ingleborough Hall, which is a school for outdoor studies. His potting shed is an artist's studio. Reginald Farrer, after whom a local nature trail is named, gave Clapham Woods distinction when he cleverly located here a tract of acid ground that would suit his beloved "rhodies."

A Bit o' Luck

When a farmer and a dealer had finished haggling over the price of stock, the palms of their hands came together with a resounding thwack. The deal was sealed without recourse to bits o' paper. It was up to the purchaser to ask for "luck," originally a silver coin. Later it represented a good deal of money which was gratefully received without troubling the Income Tax inspector.

A group of farmers, upset by a falling market for their stock and by the high prices ruling at supermarkets, are selling Dales lamb direct to the customer. They reckon the customer will pay less than if the lamb is retailed through a shop and that their income as producers will improve. In this bureaucratic age there is a flurry of forms and registered abbatoirs have to be used. Some old-timers will be recalling when they haggled over the price of farm stock and when the hand-clasp was followed by the giving of "luck" with all the certainty of night following day.

Such a way of trading was caught by BBC cameras many years ago when life at Rainscar, a big sheep farm lying "back o' Penyghent," was recorded in documentary form. Each year a dealer turned up to buy some of the best sheep. It was an anxious time for John Coates and his family. As the moment drew near when the handclasp would seal the bargain, the spectators to this ancient battle of wits looked on anxiously. Even the Dales-bred sheep that were involved in the sale seemed to sense the drama of the situation. There were some false starts. Hands were held out, close together. They wavered and were withdrawn. Then, after more fine haggling, they came together with a thwack. Everybody relaxed except the farmer, who would now be called upon to hand over "a bit o' luck."

When cattle and sheep were sold in the main streets of towns such as Hawes and Skipton, "all was filled wi' cattle an' noise," to quote Ernest Forbes, a visitor sixty years ago. There would also be a pungent smell from the assembled animals and townsfolk would have to watch where they were putting their feet. Much of the stock came from the west of Ireland and were described by one Craven grazier as "rare bee-asts: they look like nowt but fill aht surprisin' quick!"

The dealing was in sovereigns. Each farmer needed strong braces to accommodate the extra weight in his trouser pockets. For the townsfolk, the Victorian method of marketing – with cows tethered and sheep penned in the main street – was at best messy and at worst dangerous as when a lively beast broke loose and ran amok, looking for a china-shop to wreck.

A survival of that old-time trading takes place at Appleby Fair, held at the sunniest time of the year, when travelling folk come together, when trap harness is up for sale and when spotted stallions are led up and down the road so that potential buyers might assess their quality before hand-slapping seals a bargain. Dealing in horses was a chancy business. It was said that anyone who visited the (now defunct) Brough Hill fair needed to have made every mistake in the book before they attempted to deal with the visiting dealers.

There were traps for the unwary. One seller remarked, just before the handclasp, that the animal did not look very good. The prospective buyer said: "It looks aw reight to me." The horse, when purchased, turned out to be blind. The farmer said: "I telled thee it didn't look so good." A farmer who did not take good care of his horse, with the results that its ribs were showing, met the vicar who said: "I see you have the frame of a new horse in your stable." Generally, horses were well-cared-for. They had a languid time in the top pastures for a few weeks before they were needed for haytime. "Then," said one hill farmer, "they're terrible difficult to catch."

The auction mart took the cattle and sheep off the street and regularised the method of trading. The torrent of words that a good auctioneer directs at his audience would make a politician or a sports commentator green with envy. Auctioneering is a funny business. The man on the rostrum is agent for the sale until his stick whacks down, in the equivalent action to the handclasp of old, and then he becomes agent for the buyer. Ernest Forbes watched at a Dales auction mart of the 1930s as "the harassed cow is put through her paces, while around the ring loom the men of Craven; lithe, weather-beaten men with whacking sticks, all crowding over the rail and all engaged in a profound contemplation of the beast."

Forbes's auctioneer was "nimble of speech" and had "a dark, detecting eye." When his voice repeated several times the figures "twenty-four ten" there was an anguished cry from beside the ring: "Well, I'm not tekkin it!"

A Dales farmer attending an auction mart might appear naïve, even dull-witted, but a razor-sharp mind operates behind the poker face. Notice how he assesses the quality of the sheep on offer. In a swift, sure movement, he places his hand across the loin and then applies pressure to the tail root. He is determining the quality of the animal on offer. Has it got a good covering of flesh? A thick fleece might cover a multitude of ills. To an auctioneer who is selling stock, a nod is as good as a wink. A farmer, for some reason, does not like his friends to know he is bidding. The dealer is less concerned about this. The sly bidder gives a subtle movement of a finger on the crook of his stick or on the wooden stem of his tobacco pipe.

When Kit Calvert, of Hawes, was farmer, before taking over the management of the local creamery, he managed to endure the depression years of the early 1930s and, in one case, he helped a friend to pay his way. Kit arranged to take some lambs to the mart simply to get a valuation. The price offered was 16 shillings each. His friend then slaughtered the lambs, one at a time, and hawked the meat in a basket. Anything he made over 16 shillings a lamb would be split between them. The modern scheme under which enterprising farmers are collaborating to sell lamb direct to the public is an interesting variation of that devised by Kit Calvert 60 long years ago.

Auction marts are not the jolly places they once seemed to be. Then they were social as well as business occasions. Rounds of laughter shook the cafes, where farmers munched pork pies and ham sandwiches. They seemed to like their tea well-mashed, hot as hell and

black as t'fireback. Changes in farming and the food industry have
led to the closure of a number of small auction marts. With low prices,
small commissions, fewer abbatoirs and a stultifying degree of bureau-
cracy, the auction mart has become a doleful place unless it has
latched on to an aspect of livestock farming that suits the times, such
as at Skipton, where Yorkshire lamb is enthusiastically promoted.

Music-Makers

The most famous piece of music associated with the Dales is orchestral. Arthur Wood, who composed it, had associations with Harrogate, his family having moved there from Heckmondwike in 1882. He wrote a suite called "My Native Heath" and one of the movements, entitled Barwick Green, has long been renowned – as the signature tune of the long-running radio programme called "The Archers."

Arthur Wood, growing up in musical Harrogate, became organist of the Presbyterian Church at £10 a year and then got a paid job as a flautist and accompanist with the Spa orchestra. He became deputy conductor at the age of 20. Arthur recalled playing in the Valley Gardens "on cold Easter mornings when the poor chaps in the band, in top hats, blew their clarinet and cornets with running noses."

He went to London, and had a distinguished career as a theatre musician, but never forgot his northern upbringing. His wit was based on good Yorkshire sense. His daughter, Lyn recalled him coming home from a party, very proud that she had her first taste of caviare. Said father: "Acquire the taste for caviare by all means – provided you don't lose your taste for kippers." On the day before he died, he insisted – with north country stubbornness – on bringing in the coals.

Geoff Sargison, whose pleasures have included recording Dales songs and tunes, first visited the area when his father, who was a keen angler, tested his skill against the brown trout of Wensleydale. Geoff recalls venturing into Dales pubs, "perhaps a touch under age," and hearing for the first time *The Song of Swaledale*. It begins: "Land of the Swale, beautiful dale..." The occasion, very late one night, was when a group of farmers and others who were standing around the bar at the Cover Bridge Inn, burst into singing Swaledale's own special anthem. "I was amazed how well they sang it. That tune stayed with me."

Much of what Geoff has discovered about Dales music has been "on air" for he is an experienced broadcaster. A few years ago, at the time of the Swaledale Festival, he was producing an arts programme for Radio 2 which would be heard by listeners to Radio York, a station he was running at the time. He set up his equipment in the back room of a pub at Reeth. "We had to fiddle around with the transmitters. Listeners in Reeth could hear Radio Cleveland but not Radio York, which was audible on the other side of the valley. Reeth could not get Radio 2 at all!"

Geoff naturally wanted to broadcast, from the heart of Swaledale, its famous local song, which had been kept alive by the Swaledale Singers – men like Laurie Rukin of Keld – but the Dales choirs contacted by Geoff did not know it. One choir who "knew of it but had never sung it" cheerfully undertook to "get something together" for the broadcast. They got the words from one person and the tune from another source, putting them together into an acceptable piece. "We opened the programme with them standing in the pub yard, by the empty barrels, singing the Swaledale song."

Mike Harding, who is prominently associated with folk music as broadcast by Radio Two, has a house in Dentdale where, a year or two ago, Geoff arranged for a few of his friends to gather and yarn before microphones for a special tape concerned with Yorkshire Christmases. I was one of them, enjoying not only the experience but the company – Stanley Ellis and Georgina Boyes, who are dialect experts, and Juliet Barker, writer, historian and an expert on the Bronte family. The "tape" included music from all parts of Yorkshire, including the Leyburn Ladies Choir and Hawes Silver Prize Band.

The indomitable Miss Douglas, of Giggleswick, set a standard for recording Dales tunes when she toured the Craven district with folk dancers in the 1930s and persuaded old folk to demonstrate the steps of dances they performed when young and also the tunes that went with those dances. They were published in two slim books that are greatly prized by those who have personal memories of Miss Douglas and her unusual campaign.

Above: Bound for Penyghent.
Below: Racehorses heading for their morning exercise, Middleham.

Weets Cross, above Malhamdale, This is the only known example locally of a
monastic market cross that has retained its stone shaft. Elsewhere only the
bases remain.

Above: Isabel Raw and her son, Kevin, attending Swaledale sheep near Dent station.
Below: A tethered goat, Chapel-le-Dale.

Above: Bridge End, Arncliffe, where Charles Kingsley, author of *The Water-Babies,* was entertained to tea. *Below:* Barden Tower, in upper Wharfedale.

Above: A traveller's horse grazes a road verge near Garsdale Head.
Below: Reconstruction of an old-time Dales kitchen at Wensleydale Creamery, Hawes.

Above: Family outing to Ribblehead Sheep Show.
Below: A Dales collie, without which sheep farming on the fells would be impossible.

Judging a "Swardle" at Ribblehead Sheep Show, which has the celebrated viaduct as a backdrop.

Above: Pony-trekking near Malham.
Below: A village shop in Bishopdale. The shop-keeper has diversified to help combat the grim effects on rural enterprises of supermarket shopping.

A Naked Man

At Settle, in North Ribblesdale, a café bears the name Ye Olde Naked Man. It is not tucked away down one of the town's celebrated little ginnels where few people would notice it. The name is proclaimed in large lettering on a dominant building in the Market Place. How did a Naked Man come to be associated with Settle?

S D Smith, a Quaker living at Wigglesworth, delighted me for some years with a series of articles he called "Cake an' Fillin's," set in a café in a market town called Benttle. The café was the Naked Man and Benttle was an amalgam of Bentham and Settle. I remember seeing lile Mr Smith in the café when it was run by the Spencer family.

He used to pop in when he was waiting for a bus. He "filled his time wi' a sup o' summat warm." He liked "nowt better nor watching fowks from t'café winder." By eavesdropping, he soon "learned ivverybody's business. Nowt's private i' Benttle, not for long; ivverbody knows ivverybody else or somebody else'at does." Quite apart from his magazine articles, he wrote letters to the Craven Herald on topical matters. For example, when it was decided to add a chemical to the public water supply, Mr Smith, who preferred to keep the water supply as natural as possible, wondered why authority did not dump the entire contents of the local chemist's shop into the reservoir.

Ye Olde Naked Man at Settle still combines shop with café, as it did rather more than forty years ago when Mr Smith – as I always knew him – sipped tea and eavesdropped. The "naked man" features on an elaborate datestone. He holds a panel bearing the date 1663 and the initials J C, which doubtless referred to John Cookson, one of the innkeepers of the time. In the turbulent 1660s, the inns of Settle were almost too numerous to be listed. They were well supported. The population had just emerged from the stresses of the Great Civil War, when John Lambert, a Malhamdale lad who rose to high military rank under Cromwell, billeted troops in Giggleswick Church.

In the Restoration period, with Charles II as king, the Quakers fearlessly preached in Settle market place. On a December day in 1659, Samuel Watson had stood up in Giggleswick church to speak "as he was moved of God." He had his head "brok upon ye seates" before he was thrown out of the building on to the ice. Settle market boomed, packhorses followed ancient tracks across the landscape, collecting and delivering produce. There was money to spare for strong drink. Did John Cookson choose to call his inn The Naked Man for its shock value? People would surely talk about such an unusual name. Or could the name have been merely a skit against the flamboyant fashions that were coming into use?

The Naked Man – isn't! He wears a garment that fastens down his chest. The carved panel that bears the date and initials cover a saucy part of his anatomy but is presumably already covered with breeches that come down below his knees. The Naked Man holds what appears to be a plane of the medieval type, for a horizontal handle was carved at each end. The outer border seemed to one historian to resemble a Rococo coffin. He also detected what he took to be a crude indication of an X-frame chair, this being of the folding variety and of a design which, in this country, dates back to the fourteenth century.

Was the idea of the Naked Man inspired by that at Langcliffe? Dated 1660, this is marginally older. The Langcliffe effigy, known as a Naked Woman, adorned what used to be an inn. Could it have been moved when an older building was replaced with the present structure? At Langcliffe, a greater proportion of the body is covered by the panel bearing the date and two sets of initials – LSMS and CT. But does it represent a woman? Two eyes, black as grapes, stare from a rounded face. The chin has a trim beard.

A Naked Man inn existed in 1758. It is known that a meeting of people connected with the turnpike took place there in April of that year, when "mine host" was John Lawson. By 1844, the building was owned by William Calvert and the place was occupied by William Cork. It was almost certainly in the nineteenth century that the original seventeenth century building (the one bearing the datestone) had a substantial addition (which is now the shop). Notice the difference in appearance and roof levels.

In the 1880s, when Dr Charles William Buck had his home and surgery in premises now owned by Nat-West bank, an occasional visitor was Edward Elgar, who was then unknown as a composer outside his native Worcestershire but was to become one of the most celebrated. Elgar, looking from his bedroom window on to the Market Place also noticed the Naked Man sign. In that prudish age, when writing about it, he could not bring himself to use the full name but wrote in his letters N—D M-N.

Elgar entreated his friend to let him have a photograph of the inscribed stone or, if he was not prepared to do this, ask one of his young doctors to oblige. Among the effects of Dr Buck was a printed postcard of the datestone. So perhaps Elgar got his Naked Man after all.

Cooks and Bottle-washers

The first thing a man seeking employment on a Dales farm inquired about was food. He'd 'appen be content with a little less brass if he knew he was having one or two good meals each day.

A bachelor farmer in Upper Wharfedale, who worked hard and long, began each day by drinking a basinful of warm fat. He died at a ripe old age. Old-style eating would be unsuited to an age when machines do most of the hard work and when shedding weight is a major health consideration. A concerned mother said: "If our Lizzie goes on dieting it'll get to t'pitch that if she has a cuppa tea she'll look like a thermometer."

At a time of adulterated, low-calorie, prepackaged food, I listened enthralled as a fellside farmer recalled the real farmhouse fare. This was not as "fancy" as the host of television cooks would have you believe. "Half of 'em wouldn't knaw which end of a cow to milk." Country fare was satisfying but "in t'auld days there were some terrible practitioners."

We broached the subject of geese, which provided a nourishing if fatty repast and also yielded a lot of grease. His mother had rubbed goose-grease on to his chest just before he went to bed. "Tha greased thi clogs an' all wi' it. Down through t'lace holes. It stopped watter getting in." The talk switched to "butching" pigs. Every farmer kept a pig or two for family use. Each district had a pig-killer who did his job, then returned a while later to cut up the carcass. An apprentice who made a bad job of cleaving the suspended body of a pig was told by his boss: "Go easy, lad – or thou'll hev both lugs at one side."

Cutting up was a gory business. In an age before refrigerators, a family found itself with a lot of pork. The shoulders, hams and flitches were put in salt "for a fortneet or three week or summat like that." Farming families being "neighbourly," pieces of pork were distributed and in due course, when the neighbours had their pigs slaughtered, they reciprocated. "By swapping back'ard and forrard, you had fresh pork nearly all t'time."

It's your stomach that holds your back up. Porridge (usually spoken of as "poddish") was a staple food. Oatmeal was delivered by the hessian sackful. "Then we must hev gitten better off or summat, for we git Quaker Oats." Before he went to school, mother doled out some porridge in "a basin wi' three blue rings round it. (I keep coming across bits o' broken porridge basins outside). When thou'd had thi porridge, thou supped thi' tea out o' t'same basin."

It was "just same" at dinner-time (which posh folk call lunchtime). "Thou had thi taties an' meat an' stuff on a plate. And then mother would put thi rice or semolina pudding on t'same plate. Thou didn't have owt fancy like having two plates." As the pudding spread to the side of the plate, a brown ring was visible. "Pudding had shoved what were left o' t'gravy to t'outside. Thou were telled to eat it up. It were aw-reight."

My Dales friend had little respect for modern bacon. He was brought up at a time when a bacon-eater had fat dribbling from either side of his or her mouth. "Folk who buy bacon and ham today don't knaw what real bacon and ham is. But if thou hasn't had it, tha doesn't knaw, dost ta?" There was more "body" in bacon. "In them days they kept pigs for a birthday," by which he meant that a pig was not killed when it was less than a year old. "They're not so old now. There isn't such a thing as a bacon pig. It's a porker now." To him, modern bacon was "summat like brown paper."

And ham! As my friend spoke, I thought of that glorious passage from the writings of J B Priestley, when he described the elements of an old-time West Riding tea. Modern ham, I gathered, is nowt like the stuff they had then. "Thou gits it sliced and then they put it in fancy cellophone stuff. It all goes wet. When we had ham sandwiches, yon ham was twice as thick as t'breead [bread]. Ham thou gits today is like pages out o' t'Bible, it's that thin. If thou holds it up, thou can see through it. I marvel that they've found a machine to cut it that thin.

And it tastes o' nowt."

There was an intermission, as some tea was brewed. He was getting clagged [mouth-bound] with ceaseless talk. He drank deeply, then said: "Toast!" What could be wrong with modern toast? "They put thin bread in these toasting machines. We have yan. It's aw reight but it dries it reight through. Proper toast is made out o' bread thou's cut thick and then put to t'fire on a toasting fork. It just burnt t'outside." Then, I gathered, "thou ladled it wi' butter. Thou didn't put butter on and scraped it off. By – wouldn't I give owt for summat like that today."

A Wet Haytime

Jim Metcalfe, of Stainforth, gave me an at times hilarious account of a sodden haytime at Darnbrook, a big sheep farm on Malham Moor. In Jim's time, it was occupied by the Robinsons and their vast hill-going family of horned sheep.

Haytime came late at Darnbrook. The yows and lambs were kept in the meadows until well into springtime and, as Jim said, you can't have it all ways, can you? It was just after the the 1939-45 war that he gave the Robinsons a hand. Jim was not sure of the year, but he was not long out of the Royal Navy. When Mr Robinson, snr., organised a big "lead" of hay, most of the Craven farmers had got their crops safely gathered in. With a "lead" in prospect, Mr Robinson went to Skipton to engage a couple of Irishmen to help out.

Men from Co Mayo, on the west coast of Ireland, came to the Dales in quite large numbers to assist with haytime. A man was employed for a month at a fixed sum, his food and accommodation being provided, and if the weather was inclement he was put to work doing other jobs, like thistle-stubbing or whitewashing out the buildings, which was known as "bug-blinding." Mr Robinson drove his Irishmen to Darnbrook at the best possible speed. They shuddered at finding themselves truly in the wilds and in an area that lay about 1,000 ft above the level of the Irish Sea.

They were allocated a bedroom. One man pepped [peeped] from the window into the garden, where a weeping ash was growing. He said to his pal: "Patrick – what a queer world we've come to live in. The trees are growing downhill."

Jim was summoned to Darnbrook by Norman, "the oldest of the Robinson lads" who had said: "We're terribly late wi' haytime. We've eaten it too hard in t'spring and we've been late at mowing. We got War-Ag to mow it and they knocked down forty-odd acre. And looked at t'weather..." Now Darnbrook had over eighty acres of meadowland, so when Jim arrived t'biggest half of t'grass was still unmown. He joined forces with the family, with Tommy Towler, a farm man who had married Mary Robinson, and the Irishmen.

Rain continued to fall as though from a celestial hosepipe. "I was there three weeks before I cast my eyes on t'field. We never went near it. Grass that had been cut had nearly gone out of sight as t'fog [second flush of grass] grew through." One day, as the men were pointing some masonry at an outbuilding, the sun showed its face. It was doubtless a flash in the pan. Jim thought it was going to take up. Others were not so sure. "They'd lost heart wi' t'job." As the weather continued to look promising, they decided to tackle the first meadow. "All the grass mown weeks before was now well and truly out of sight, swamped by fog-grass."

The men had a hand-rake apiece. When Frank Caton came up from Otterburn to help, and he asked where the hay was to be found, he was told that when he got into t'field he'd find plenty. The only way to separate the old swathes from the lusty growth of fresh grass was to strike twice with the rake in the same spot. It was tedious work. They began at the wallside and had not been long at the job when Mary Robinson appeared at the field gate and shouted "Dinner time!"

The men, who were at the far side of the meadow, decided they would "work their way back," taking "longest way round" till they reached the gate. It took them an hour and a-half. The hay they pulled out was, said Jim, "as red as a fox – no good." They kept it none the less, putting it inside the barn. "It wasn't worth much but up at Darnbrook it'd keep summat alive." Happily, the largest proportion of the crop was good hay. "So it made up for t'disappointment of t'first lot."

The Iron Road

The train now standing at Hawes Station is going – nowhere. It is the most conspicuous object at the Dales Countryside Museum, reminding us of Hawes Joint Station and the forty-mile Wensleydale railway of beloved memory. The line was special, using a broad gap in the north-west barrier of the high Pennines to link the North-East main line with Garsdale, formerly known as Hawes Junction, on the Settle-Carlisle line.

The steam train has become an object of romance. For those who habitually used steam-hauled trains, the experience of rail travel in big towns or cities included standing on draughty platforms that reeked of soot and fish. The creases were taken from your clothes as, with the arrival of a locomotive and a release of steam, you were enveloped in damp greyness. In the steam age, passengers had to perform surreptitious acts of dry-cleaning or use the corner of a handkerchief to remove a speck from an eye.

Hawes, being a rural station, was spared the soot-and-fish tang, which was swept away by a "lazy" wind that tried to cut through you. In summer, there was the all-pervading flavour of new-mown hay. The locomotive that is now on view is an ex-industrial tanker, conveyed to the Museum on a low-loader, to be put on display thinly disguised as British Railways No 67345, which was one of the last locomotives to operate on the Wensleydale line.

In its heyday, Hawes was a despatch point for dressed stone from the Burtersett quarries to the burgeoning Lancashire cotton towns. Roadmen tore their hair when they saw the damage caused by heavy, horse-drawn carts and slippers [a braking device] on the descent from Burtersett to the main road. Hawes was also an important collecting centre for milk from the outlying farms. The milk arrived in large kits on horse-drawn traps. Sometimes, a race between traps led to one of them colliding with a gate stoop. Now the old station yard is a car park.

The Midland and North-Eastern Railway jointly operated the station at Hawes from its inception in 1878 and at Garsdale the North-Eastern had a small engine shed constructed mainly of sleepers. It burnt down at the edge of living memory. I chatted with an old lady who was a child at the time. She remembered the great excitement among the residents of the railway cottages who awoke to find a lurid glow in the sky.

Garsdale was as wild a spot as you might find. In my monograph on the station, I recalled when Ernest Forbes, artist and newspaper cartoonist, was a visitor in August 1931. He used the small ridge and furrow canopy of the main station building as an umbrella as rain slanted down. Then, reaching for his sketching pad and pencil, he drew his impression of the isolated station and captioned the picture "Two Hours to Go."

Two people shared his draughty quarters. On his Yorkshire tour, Forbes had a friend and at what is now called Garsdale station – it was then Hawes Junction – they met a man from Dent and were amused by his manner and dialect, which Forbes painstakingly wrote down. The man's father was "ovver eighty-five, an' he's getten all 'is faculties. There's nowt 'e don't remember!" Forbes had been told that a Leeds train would leave the station at 10.22 a.m. "And if we missed that, a guileless friend assured us, there were trains dashing through every two or three minutes."

They arrived at the station with two or three minutes to spare, to find that "the 10.22 had always left at 10.15 and that since the 20th of July it had left at 10.5." It seemed to Forbes that "most of the trains that dashed into Hawes Junction as quickly dashed out again – so quickly, indeed, that no live man could catch them."

The first time I used the Wensleydale line from Garsdale, I was travelling in the Bradford-Hawes express that was nicknamed Bonnyface. This was the only train between Hawes and Garsdale that ran on time. As the distance between the two places was six miles, timekeeping was not difficult.

One train is said to have been driven the six miles back from Hawes to Garsdale in six minutes, at a time when carriages were not well sprung. The passengers did not seem to mind the jolting. The alternative form of transport was horse and wagonette.

Years ago, in chats with Annie Mason of Hawes, I heard of the time when James Pratt, her father, who was a well-known cattle dealer, was taken by horse and trap to Garsdale station when a train was stopped for him. The Midland regarded Mr Pratt as an important customer. The cattle he bought were transported back to the dale by train.

The last time I travelled on the Wensleydale line was also the most unusual. Being the only passenger at Garsdale, I was invited to join the crew on the footplate. "Keep thi' eeard down when we come to a station or we'll cop it," said the convivial driver. Those were the days when rural stationmasters were smartly uniformed and had "scrambled egg" on the brim of their caps. At each station, one of them peered intently into the carriages, saw no one and signalled the driver to proceed. The only passenger was travelling with the crew.

A man who recalled boyhood visits from Northallerton to his grandparents at Leyburn knew the train as the Hawes Express. It was "a small tank engine that usually seemed to travel in reverse." He remembered railway sounds – the much-clattering of milk kits, squawking of hens in crates and, at times, "the sad sob of a little calf sewn up in sacking."

Passenger services from Hawes to Northallerton ended in April 1954. The branch from Hawes to Garsdale was closed down in March 1959, though a rail link was maintained east of Redmire quarries for the transport of limestone until 1992. The so-called last train on tracks that terminated at Redmire was a special from King's Cross that was planned to run on January 2nd. I would have loved to be among the bustling commuters at King's Cross when the name of diminutive little Redmire boomed out over the loudspeakers.

I visited Fingall, a typical country station, to await the arrival of what was generally considered to be the last goods train, a Class 60 diesel locomotive hauling a rake of empty wagons that would be exchanged for full ones. Fingall station had been distinguished a few years before, being filmed for one of the BBC productions based on the James Herriot books, the series having the general title of "All Creatures Great and Small". A local man mentioned that the first intimation local people had about the filming was the appearance of a phone box – a television "prop" that looked most convincing until someone saw some outdated equipment, with buttons marked A and B.

The filming was a triumph of deception. Railings were painted brown. The script had been so written that the arrival and departure of a train was presumed, a "steam machine" providing the cloud of vapour. The train noises, such as the hissing of escaping steam and clattering of the carriages over rail joints, would be dubbed on to the sound-track. The cameras were set-up on the trackbed. I heard from Fingall folk what happened during the 1940s, a time when young Alf Wight, alias James Herriot began his veterinary work. With a world war raging, ammunition trains used the line and "every bit o' decent waste land and roadside in this district had ammunition dumped on it."

Mist as damp and chilling as a dish-clout enveloped the valley when the last passenger train appeared from the murk, the first of three diesel locomotives bearing the name "The Wensleydale Lament." I dashed on to Redmire, where the local people stared with disbelief as the special train disgorged its hundreds of railway fans. The mist had drifted away. Everything was revealed with clarity and colour. Old railwaymen, their eyes misting, related stories of the line. Photographers stood in good-natured lines as though on a military manoevre.

As the "last train" began its return journey, the mist returned. Three fog detonators placed on the tracks were detonated by the leading locomotive – an appropriate railway tribute to a passing age. The train squealed to a halt so that the key-token could be transferred to the cab of the leading diesel. The man who effected the transfer did so with a stately walk. Everyone looked. No one spoke.

Skipton

On the Buses

Orange-sided Pennine buses are still a familiar sight on the Skipton-Giggleswick route. In the heyday of the firm, buses ran to Lancaster. The first timetable was based on the need for a Gargrave schoolmistress to travel to her work at Coniston Cold – and to be there in good time.

Just over 50 years ago, I commuted from Skipton to Clapham by Pennine bus. It was invariably crowded and there was a conductress to take the money and to ensure that the bus was not overloaded. Sometimes, the crush was such that we almost had to take turns to breathe. In the days when many farmers travelled by bus, we knew when it was muck-spreading time. In springtime, nearly every road-side meadow had its nesting pair of curlews. When the door opened in summer, there was the smell of new-mown hay rather than petrol fumes. One day, one passenger was a goat. I was also to see a calf wrapped in sacking and owned by a man who left the bus at Hellifield and headed for the auction mart.

Edgar Smith recalled for me the early days of a characterful bus company. The Pennine began in 1926, when Jim Windle bought a 20 h.p., 14-seater *Overland* bus and drove it on the Skipton-Settle route. The first passenger to travel from Gargrave to Coniston Cold was a schoolteacher, Bertha McKell, so the bus service fitted in to her routine. Jim continued to run that single machine until, in 1927, when the district was on the line of totality for an eclipse of the sun and thousands of people flooded into the area by road and rail.

Jim realised the potential of the service. A proper timetable was needed and more than one bus was needed to sustain it. He contacted the Simpson brothers, Arthur and Vic, who helped him with finance. The second bus was similar to the first. Arthur Simpson, an excellent mechanic, who had tinkered with motor cycles, became involved in the firm, attending to mechanical matters at the large garage behind the Grouse Hotel at Gargrave. In the beginning, cheap petrol was purchased from ROP (Russian Oil Products) which became LPD (Lancashire Petrol Distributors, originating at Preston).

The bus fleet was augmented by as 26-seater *Starflier* and two Leyland *Lionesses*, which had a similar capacity. In 1928, Pennine took delivery of two forward-drive Leyland *Lions*, which were 30-seaters. Jim needed some extra drivers, to be based on Settle, and among the new-starters was Tommy Faulker. When Edgar Smith joined the Pennine in 1930, Jim was no longer driving; he occupied an office at Gargrave and supervised the running of the firm.

The orange colour of the buses became a distinctive feature of the company following a visit to Leyland, in Lancashire, to purchase a new vehicle. When they were asked to make a choice of colour, they elected for that of one of the firm's buses, which was being used to transport the football team to matches. Orange contrasted with the various shades of red favoured by other local bus companies, such as Ribble and West Yorkshire.

The Pennine enterprise extended its range to Ingleton by taking over a route used by the Lamb family of Settle, who had a *Minerva*, a most stylish bus. Lambs had some lorries operating from quarries at Ingleton. Petrol for them was transported on an early bus out of Settle. Disaster struck when it was crossing Newby Moor (which is better known as Clapham Common). The bus caught fire and burnt out. The bus service of the Lambs ended, so Jim Windle decided to run his Pennine stock to Ingleton, where he met up with County Motors from Lancaster. There was a switch of passengers who were travelling the full distance. When Ribble took over, Jim countered by sending Pennine buses through to Morecambe.

Edgar told me that the Pennine evolved at the same time as the Craven Pothole Club. The potholers had begun to make rope ladders and for a journey to Alum Pot, in North Ribblesdale, they paid Alan Stephenson 30s for the loan of his car, which was a bull-nosed Morris, a four-seater open tourer. When the tackle had been stowed, only two people could be accommodated. Alum Pot was descended and on the way back to Skipton, they "bounced" into the yard at the back of the Golden Lion and the car developed a spring-shackle fault. Spanners were borrowed and repairs effected.

Edgar then asked Jim Windle if the club might use one of the Pennine buses. Jim agreed to the plan, adding: "If thou'll drive it for nowt, thou can have it for thirty shillings." The first outing, to Sell Gill, in 1929, was by an enthusiastic company of potholers, plus the celebrated Tot Lord of Settle, antiquary, caver and a man associated with the infant cave rescue organisation. He was "picked up" in Settle.

The *Overland* bus, with its full complement of cavers and a mass of tackle on the roof, was driven along the green lane from Horton to beyond the beck at Sell Gill, where Edgar turned it round and parked it up. Tot, who was rather a plump character, could not always be persuaded to go underground. The *Overland* was used by the potholers until it was decided to scrap it. The potholers then went out and about in style using a *Lioness*. Edgar was known as "Limestone Smith" to the members.

He recalls that when workmen digging a hole for an electricity pole on the low ground near Long Preston came across a pair of horns from a primeval ox, they were immediately claimed by Tot, who set off with this cumbersome burden to walk from Long Preston to his home in Settle. Edgar had to refuse Tot's request to let him board the bus with the horns as hand-luggage.

The Pennine company operates as far as Giggleswick but has extended its range into West Craven. On my old-time journeys, I could book to Clapham. En route, we crossed Buckhaw Brow, which then had a steeper gradient near the top. I remember hearing the story of a motorist who had parked at the top of the Brow and asked the garage proprietor if the hill was dangerous. He replied: "Not up here – it's down at bottom where they all kills thersens."

Forty years ago, when there was little road traffic in the Dales, a West Yorkshire bus en route from Grassington to Ilkley stopped at Barden. The driver and conductor, having five minutes to spare, responded to the heat of the day and dosed off. Neither woke until after the time the bus should have been at its destination, about eight miles away. This was told to me when I was researching the story of the red-painted buses. At Appletreewick (known to local folk as Aptrick) the bus was being driven up the steep main street when the conductor, John Brotherton, told the driver he had a parcel to deliver at the post office. "Don't bother stopping," he remarked. "Just slow down and I'll step off. You can stop at the top of the hill." The conductor tramped to the hilltop only to discover that the bus had gone without him. He thumbed a lift in a van and caught up with the bus at Barden.

When J W Ward presided over the Grassington depot, he told me that one summertime a Leeds driver, in the run over Kidstones Pass to Wensleydale, encountered a free-ranging bull. He stopped the bus and waited for the animal to amble away. Instead, it walked up to the bus, sniffed the radiator, stepped back a pace or two and then charged. Both headlamps were shattered. Horn marks covered the paintwork along the front of the bus.

Life was rarely humdrum for the crews of Service 127, a thirty-mile run between Ripon and Hawes that was operated by United from 1930. Unbelievably, in days when petrol pumps were few and far between, the service extended from Harrogate via Hawes to Ingleton. When Tabby Cove's bus ran out of petrol between the last two places, he walked seven miles back to Hawes for a supply. J-type buses had pneumatic tyres and two doors, both on the nearside. The conductor rang the bell to alert the driver by pulling on a rope. A wooden block was used as a chock on the steeper hills. At Howgate Bank, Askrigg, the passengers had to walk and the bus was "chocked" yard by yard as it roared slowly uphill.

Poultry in hampers, boxes of eggs and also rabbits were among the rural produce that passengers took to town on market day. In the 1920s, baskets containing eggs and hampers holding chickens might be stacked on top of the bus; more baskets of eggs were placed on the huge bonnet. It is a wonder they were not cooked during the journey. If a low branch swept the top of the bus, some hampers fell off and the crew chased any hens and chickens that were tasting freedom. The company charged for excess luggage when passengers began to bring the produce of others as well as their own.

When Wensleydale was served by the Northallerton Omnibus Service, a cattle dealer from West Witton approached the bus and asked the conductor if he could bring along a calf. Although the bus was packed, the conductor agreed. The dealer went off to collect the animal. He was back, ten minutes later, with a half-grown stirk he was leading on a cord. Attempts were made to push the stirk through the back door, but they were unsuccessful. The mission was aborted.

Black Game

Gurt Bill, who lived by the upper Swale, remembered when, at snowtime, there might be over a hundred hungry black grouse ravaging the fellside thorn trees for berries. A blackcock, male of the species, was a solid bird that was good to eat. There were three different colours o' flesh – pink, then white, then rather dark. "I was nivver particular how it was cooked; it always seemed to taste good!"

The speedy decline of the black grouse on the Northern Pennines is a matter of grave concern. One of two birds might be seen around Langthwaite in Arkengarthdale, and rather more have been counted around Langdon Beck, in Teesdale. Otherwise, you must look hard and long for a glimpse of this splendid bird.

The last blackcock I saw was on a berried thorn tree near Dent railway station, which stands well over 1,000 feet above sea level. It was bitingly cold. The thin winter sunlight gave the blackcock's dark plumage some silvery highlights. In the dale-country, a black grouse was mostly seen in thinly-wooded areas with plenty of ground cover rather than on open moorland, the haunt of its smaller cousin, the red grouse. It was the sort of country that Fred Lawson, the Wensleydale artist, thought about when first he moved into the Dales. He had wanted to live near "those scraggy bits at the edge of moors where there is water rushing down into the valley."

Forty years ago, I took "black game" for granted. Birds abounded between Teesdale and Weardale. I scarcely failed to see some whenever I motored along a little used road through a tousled countryside between Langdon Beck and St John's Chapel. If I was travelling between Keld and Tan Hill at first or last light in spring, I might see birds at their tourney ground, known as the *lek*, and hear calls that seemed like echoes from prehistory, including cooing sounds and occasional explosive hisses. This *lek* was near West Stonesdale where, most recently, a pair of blackcock were displaying to each other on the road verge, under the excited eyes of a naturalist who had parked nearby.

That was the district in which Gurt Bill, whose real name was William Alderson, had grown up. What are silent hills today then resounded to the fluting of the curlew, to the goat-like bleating of the snipe and also to the melancholic whistling of the golden plover. Enter the territory of a redshank and the resident male would call with such shrillness it might be proclaiming the end of the world.

Upland waders as well as black grouse are less numerous than they were. The number of displaying blackcocks has declined from 25,000 in the early nineteen-nineties to rather more than 6,000 birds. The loss of suitable habitat is held mainly responsible. Land improvement, over-grazing by sheep and the planting of dense tracts of conifers have had a startling effect on the vegetation.

Efforts to redress the situation are being made by the North Pennine Black Grouse Recovery Project, which was established in 1996. Demonstration sites have been set up to show landowners the bird's preferred habitat and so that such conditions can be created to enable the population to recover. Re-introduction is a chancy business. In the 1860s, eggs set under domestic hens hatched out and the black-game chicks were released into the Bowland district. In two or three years, the birds had disappeared.

Arthur Gilpin, the Leeds ornithologist, and authority on Yorkshire birds, believed that at the start of the nineteenth century blackgame were scarce in Yorkshire and they continued to be uncommon until about the 1850s when, partly because of introductions, they became reasonably common from Swale to Wharfe. By the 1970s, when I was first interested in black grouse, the Bowland stock had declined, mainly because their territories had been swamped by conifers. A big *lek* in what became known as Gisburn Forest broke up through tree-planting, though for a time several smaller *leks* were known.

Before the catchment area of Stocks reservoir, in the upper Hodder Valley, was blanketed by conifer trees, I watched swaggering blackcocks secure territories within the *lek* and, when a greyhen appeared, reach a state of great excitement. It was at the *lek*, in the majority of cases, that mating took place. The female, known as a greyhen, must then find a nesting site, make the nest, lay and incubate eggs and attend to the chicks without masculine help.

I have watched black grouse *lekking* on the rough ground beyond Beckermonds, where two mountain becks meet to form the River Wharfe. The map indicates a a related feature, this being Cocklet Hill. My own special area of study was on "white" moorland above Malhamdale – the sort of grassy terrain that contrasted with "black" ground, which is peat and heather.

drawn by David Binns

Stan Lythe, of Grassington, had found a tourney ground in the off-season. He recognised it because here the vegetation had been pounded by the feet of displaying grouse until it resembled coconut matting. He put up a hide – and in the following April I was invited to join him to observe the antics of displaying blackcock as they secured the best possible territories and, through competition, brought themselves into peak breeding condition.

The best display was at break of day. A somewhat less intense demonstration took place in the late afternoon up to the end of April. I opted for this time because of the improved chance of obtaining photographs. Stan said the black grouse would arrive at a little before four o'clock – and so they did, responding to a diurnal clock that in a short time brought birds from different directions to one little patch of ground.

The first intimation I had was when I heard a loud *tchie-whai*, close to the hide. The sound was like air rushing from a bicycle tyre when the valve was suddenly removed. Or could it have been an avian sneeze? I peered through one of the flaps to see the turkey-like bird a few yards away and just a few feet from another cock bird that faced it and was similarly noisy and excited. A displaying bird seemed twice as big as usual. As it "sneezed" the head and bill pointed upwards and the breast was puffed out. The lyre-shaped tail was fanned out, revealing the brilliant white of the under-tail coverts, and the wings were drooped. I fancied that the red wattles had been expanded.

Another prominent sound was a pigeon-like cooing, uttered when a bird was standing with distended throat and wings and tail quivering. I took the "sneeze" to be a challenge to the facing cock bird and the dove-like cooing to represent an attempt to hold on to or improve a bird's territorial rights, for the performance was all about territory. The best territories were at the centre of the *lek*.

A visiting greyhen was inclined to pitch down at the edge of the area, causing great excitement among the assembled cock birds. She would then scutter towards the centre, where she might permit herself to be courted and mated by a bird at the middle of the *lek* or depart, causing excitement among the blackcocks. Gilpin recorded that when a greyhen was present, he had seen cock birds throw themselves more than a foot into the air and strike out with their claws like gamecocks.

The display seemed to lose its impetus after about half an hour. Soon the area was deserted by the grouse – until dawn, when the ancient ritual would be re-enacted.

Gone from most of the dale-country are the winter packs of black-game remembered by Girt Bill. Birds that frequented the roadside thorn trees for berries along the roadside between Settle and Scosthrop were vulnerable to those who were inclined to shoot them from a car.

The Highest Pub

For thirty-four years, Susan Peacock, a wispy woman of Dales stock, presided over the inn on Tan Hill. These were England's highest licensed premises, being at an elevation of 1,732 feet. Susan told inquirers that she was too busy to be lonely, though she would leave her remote home to attend the funeral of an acquaintance, or to visit Muker Show. She looked forward to having a springtime shopping jaunt to Darlington.

Susan was a frontierswoman – the type of person who, if she had been born in American fifty or so years earlier, would have been found sitting in the driving seat of a covered wagon going west across the prairie. Instead, she went north to Tan Hill in 1903 as the wife of Richard Parrington and mother of three daughters. She was twice married and on her death at Tan Hill in 1937 she was survived by her second husband, Michael Peacock, and daughter Edna. They left the famous hostelry in 1945.

One of my visits to Tan Inn was on a late winter's day that had a springtime feel about it. The sky was (untypically) blue. The air was (untypically) calm. Each lofty Pennine ridge was banded by snow – the cores of old drifts. Holding a camera, I walked backwards along the Pennine Way, concentrating on achieving a good photographic balance between the inn and the wilderness. I spun round, to take a second picture, and collided with a Pennine Way signpost, which was the only vertical object on a 10,000-acre grouse moor.

Several stars briefly joined the wisp of moon in the clear blue sky above Tan Hill. A cock grouse breasted the wind, climbing steeply, as though to have a better look at this careless human. The grouse settled down to a round of coarse shouting, *kowa, kowa, kok, kok, kok*. At the inn, "mine host", who then was Alec Baines, provided me with a cup of coffee and some soothing ointment for my wound.

Later, standing on the outcropping gritstone behind Tan Hill inn, near the meeting place of unfenced roads from Swaledale, Arkengarthdale and the Eden Valley, I saw the place in its wild context. My eyes ranged over immense distances to some of the Pennine giants – to Great Shunner Fell, High Seat and Nine Standards Rigg. The nearest neighbour was almost four miles away. And I thought of a lady who presided over the highest inn in the land and enjoyed the "quiet places."

If the spirit of Susan Peacock still frequents Tan Hill, she will be aware of many changes. The coal pits have closed. The once-rutted roads that converge near the isolated building now have a durable surface. With the boundary changes of 1974, Tan Hill was transferred into county Durham but has since returned to the Yorkshire fold. The inn is much bigger than it was and double-glazing ensures that it is no longer a playground for draughts.

Tales are told of past tenants who, like Susan, had to face up to the worst the weather might give. Recent winters have been tropical in comparison. One "mine host" went outdoors on a winter day to collect some coal for the fire and returned to find that the front door had frozen shut. He had to break a window to gain admittance to his home. In the absence of a beer-cellar it was sufficient to keep the ale in a breeze-block garage. The 1985-6 winter piled snow and ice against the walls to such effect the place resembled an igloo. Ice up to four inches thick covered the windows, effectively cutting out the daylight.

I had known of Susan Peacock from old books and yellowing newspaper cuttings. Tales about this indomitable landlady were given to me by Laurie Rukin of Keld, Bill Alderson of Angram and Donald Lee (better known to his friends as Gig), a cyclist who had visited Tan Hill between the wars. Susan was born at West Witton, in Wensleydale. She left school to find employment "keeping house" for a farmer at Swineside, Coverdale, and she was then in service with a farming family in Craven. Dickie Parrington, whom she married, was licensee of the Cat Hole inn at Keld before taking over at Tan Hill.

When Dickie cocked his clogs [died] Susan married a roadman

who had been born in Arkengarthdale and she became Mrs Peacock. Of the three daughters, Maggie married and moved to Oxford, Olive became the wife of a Wensleydale farmer and Edna, who remained single, worked for the Bagshaws at Low Row Post Office until, on her mother's death, she returned to Tan Hill to "keep house" for her stepfather.

In the 1930s, with Susan firmly in control, an aura of romance lay about Tan Hill Inn as a result of newspaper articles and wireless broadcasts. Susan was persuaded to talk about her life "in quite places." On an exciting occasion, she joined the Swaledale Singers in a broadcast from Leeds. The four singers were paid two guineas each for their contribution. Susan was "a shade nervous" at first but was soon made to feel at ease. She was not attracted to the wireless and remarked that her husband, Michael, was "not struck on it either."

A London visitor to Tan Hill wrote in the visitors' book for 1935: "Broadcasting now has made Tan Hill famous all England o'er, so what a joy to find it still as simple as before." A journalist found that even her experience as a star on t'wireless had not robbed her of "her simple homeliness and transparent sincerity. She is not the picturesque and romantic person which many townspeople who heard her broadcast last week imagine her to be. The isolation of the inn is really only in a geographical sense and scores of motorists who visit Tan Hill on Sundays create a constant link between the inn and the rest of the world."

Susan underplayed the hardships of life at the back o' beyond, even the time when the chimney was blown down and, on another day, when Michael "came round t'side of t'building on his hands and knees." She was not only used to life in wild places but preferred it to village life. In 1935, a reporter who spent an hour or two at the inn saw a caller who, leading a stallion from Whitaside to Bowes, was in need of refreshment, a request that set Susan "frying ham and brewing tea." A hiker stopped for a pint. Another caller was a motor-cyclist from "Teesdale side." The three visitors turned up "in the middle of Mrs Peacock's baking day." Susan, scared o' naebody, none the less kept a loaded revolver in the house. It was pointed at the knockabout man [tramp] who demanded something to eat and refused to leave.

Susan could be well-disposed to lowly folk, one of whom, known as Tan Hill Joe, was courting "an oldish woman" from Reeth, which was not easy, for he had to do so through correspondence and could neither read nor write. His "love letters" were written by Susan, who would simply put some obvious sentiments and then ask him "is there owt else tha wants to put in t'letter?" When a reply was received, it was Susan who read it to him. A courtship mainly conducted by post had a satisfactory consequence. They eventually "wed."

In Susan's time, Tan Hill inn was a place of dark oak and gleaming brass. She kept a good fire and there was a substantial fender, about two feet high, with a cushion round the top. "You sat on it and warmed your back before the fire." Mr Parrot, headmaster at Kirkby Stephen, was a keen cricketer who bussed two teams to Tan Hill one summer evening. On the way up, the cricketers had some fun picking wild flowers. Susan Peacock was invited to judge which was the best bunch. She did so with enjoyment. It was the start of the Tan Hill Flower Show, which ran for years.

One of my informants about the lady who presided over the highest inn "forgit what Susan's last ailment was" adding "but she didn't lig lang. She went fairly sharpish at t'finish." The funeral was the largest every seen in those parts. Forty cars were in the procession from Tan Hill Inn to the kirkyard at Keld, where she was laid to rest. Donald Lee, who as an energetic cyclist had covered the dale-country thoroughly and had stayed at any number of farmhouses and cottages, had never – during Susan's time – managed to spend a night at the inn. With her death, this became possible.

He recalled for me lying in a high bed with "brass knobs on." In the tiny bedroom was a water jug and basin for washing purposes. Next morning, he arose, wandered around the inn and, meeting no one, went outside to find Edna returning with a yoke on her shoulders to support two pails full of water she had drawn from a spring beside the Arkengarthdale road. Such was the origin of the inn's drinking water.

Another time, there was the morning knock at the bedroom door and the discovery just outside the door of a container with hot water for shaving. Opening the door was memorable because he was assailed by the appetising smell of home-fed bacon being cooked. "They had a hen or two and you allus got a couple of eggs."

A Dales Farm

Just Rambling

Alfred Wainwright compiled his hand-written guides to our northern fells at the rate of one page per evening. He broke off his work only to feed the cat and to watch "Coronation Street" on television. It reminded him of his mill-town background. His earliest fell-wandering was done using public transport. He walked in old clothes, with studded boots on his feet.

They used to call someone who walked long distances for pleasure a "hiker." A posher term was "rambler." He was something more than a pedestrian. The Victorians who formed the Yorkshire Ramblers' Club climbed mountains and were pioneer potholers. Alfred Wainwright, the Blackburn lad who had a vision of Heaven when he stood for the first time on a Lakeland peak and beheld a wonderland of mountains and lakes, also knew the Pennine Dales well.

In the late 1930s, he strode by dale and fell, from Settle to Hadrian's Wall, and wrote an account of his experiences. It was published half a century later, when he had become celebrated as the man who devised new-style walking guides featuring tidy drawings and puckish as well as perceptive text. I recall in particular his comment that it was vital for a person new to rambling to be able to tell the difference between a ripe bilberry and a fresh sheep dropping.

AW travelled light. At butty-time, he had a sandwich or two. He was "partial" to fish and chips. When he was persuaded to appear in the radio series *Desert Island Discs*, it was on condition that it was recorded in Manchester (not London) and that afterwards he would be taken to Harry Ramsden's fish and chip emporium at Guiseley.

His original idea when compiling a guide to the fells was to use it as a "memory hook" in old age. When his leg muscles had stiffened and his breath came in the proverbial short pants, he would glance at it and let his imagination take him back to the high and lonely places. His work was published. He became a cult figure – almost, indeed, the patron saint of ramblers. Ironically, towards the end of his life he could not fully appreciate his drawn and written work because of defective vision.

Another fell-walking friend, Charlie Emett, has recorded his north-country walks in twenty guide books. Charlie's eyesight has remained keen, though one of his walking pals, Bill Bamlett, had trouble with his vision but did not let this deter him from following Charlie along high paths and sheep-trods. When I last met Charlie, on the village green at Reeth in Swaledale, his footwear looked cracked and care-worn. Over the last few years, he'd walked through five pairs of boots. One pair lasted him for 1,700 miles before falling to pieces.

Snoopy, his toy poodle, was still light on its suspension despite thir-teen years of brisk fell-trotting. "He's a real little character," said his owner, as we set off from Reeth towards Fremington Edge and the hamlet of Booze. A clanging noise in Charlie's haversack was not a cow-bell but Snoopy's feeding dish, which was rubbing against anoth-er metallic object.

Charlie was brought up by a grandmother at Kirkby Stephen. He has boyhood memories of visiting relates in Swaledale. Aunt Harriet married a Hutchinson, who was inn-keeper and farmer at the famous Cathole, near Keld. The hostelry was famous for ham and egg break-fasts. "In those days," said Charlie, "Swaledale was very lonely. Aunt Harriet endured the long dark nights and was really glad when spring – and the first visitors – arrived. Swaledale folk liked a good crack [gossip] and you can't do that if there's nobody to talk with!"

On our way to Booze, Charlie had a tale to tell about every local feature, even about Calver, one of the least-known hills in the Dales. He and his walking pals had descended from the hill in a cloudburst. By the time they reached an inn, they were soaked to the skin and water was spurting from their boots. They were greeted by some hol-idaymakers as "proper walkers."

From the hamlet of Booze, where there were drifts of yellow moun-tain pansies, we followed a moorland way, then descended through big old woods that rang with the laughter of green woodpeckers. A path led us to the "watering hole" at Langthwaite and through a succession of fields (and over a variety of stiles) back to Reeth. Snoopy was being carried. Charlie was still lively and his boots, though cracked and scuffed, were still clinging to his feet.

I am a Fellow of an exclusive and somewhat eccentric walking club, known as the Geriatric Blunderers. The Fellowship was awarded to me "in recognition of long and meritorious service as scribe, videoist and accomplished blunderer." We were founded with a membership of four and the original four endure, with Betty Wainwright (widow of the hallowed AW) as president. She provides us with afternoon tea at least once a year.

We have blundered from Coast to Coast, through midge-ridden areas of Scotland, around Derbyshire, along Hadrian's Wall and also the Cleveland Way. We have, of course, trodden on almost every footpath in the Dales. A recent walk was a moderate nine miles, beginning and ending at Helwith Bridge and sharing the summit of Penyghent with a large party of schoolchildren from Meanwood, Leeds. I had arranged for us to park our cars near the Helwith Bridge Hotel, which would be useful when we hobbled in, with tongues like sandpaper, at the end of the walk.

We followed Long Lane, a green road that is an eastern continuation of Thwaite Lane at Clapham and Austwick. The lane took us directly towards the nose-end of Penyghent. Our route offered panoramic views of North Ribblesdale, and especially of Moughton Fell, which has been re-shaped and terraced by quarrying. A reported bird call turned out to be the *beep, beep, beep* of a lorry reversing at the quarry but later one of the first skylarks of the year filled the air with its warbling song while hovering like a feathered helicopter. What Arthur Raistrick used to call "the blunt pyramid" of Penyghent when seen from the south seemed to fill half the sky as Long Lane lost its flanking walls and, on reaching the open fell, joined the Pennine Way. Up the well-used path from Brackenbottom came a score of brightly-clad city youngsters.

Once, we had to climb the final stretch, on the Yoredale series of rocks, with unstable scree slopes under our boots. Now there was a sort of staircase composed of local stones. The "stairway" led us to the darker millstone grit at the summit. W A Poucher, a celebrated mountain photographer of the 1930s, ascended Penyghent in 1912 and found "an armchair depression in the towering wall of gritstone" that "afforded me a comfortable seat on which to eat my lunch." Penyghent is said to be a Celtic name meaning "hill of the winds." A middle-aged couple who climbed it stood at 2,273ft and looked around. What would they say about the lofty surroundings? The lady remarked; "Wouldn't this make a good drying ground for clothes?"

Penyghent has what I consider to be the finest panoramic view of any northern hill. The view takes in Morecambe Bay and the peaks of Lakeland, which are some fifty miles away. You have a fine-weather view of Wild Boar Fell and those in the vicinity of Swaledale. At the back of Penyghent lies Fountains Fell, with the isolated farm of Rainscar on a little knoll. We descended to Horton and found the riverside path that would take us back to Helwith Bridge. The Blunderers thus entered the final stage of the walk. It had been, in Bob's recollection, "abominably wet." And so it was. What should have been a green track was partly under water.

Bob deduced that a rumbling sound was not from someone's stomach but marked the approach of a goods train. He stood in a classic spot for Settle-Carlisle photographer, which is where the railway crosses the Ribble on a metal bridge, with Penyghent forming an attractive backdrop, now resembling a lion in recline. There passed, at no more than 40 miles an hour, an EWS loco (No 66011) with a rake of laden coal trucks. The loco gleamed in the cold winter light.

The Black Stuff

In great-grandad's day, coal was what you got, at much cost of effort, from thin seams in the Yoredale series of rocks. It was poor stuff that, when burnt, sizzled and spat. You had to be desperate for money to work in a bell-pit. You had to have run out of peat or wood to burn Dales coal.

Dales coal was variable in quality and appearance. At Tan Hill, where "crow coal" was mined – and warmed the ageing limbs of Lady Anne Clifford at her Edenvale castles – there was a brown variety that had a particular value for blacksmiths. It did not "cake" in the forge. Gurt Bill, whose Sunday name was William Alderson, remembered entering one of the small pits, having clambered into a tub that was drawn underground by a pony.

The illumination was a candle attached to a piece of clay. The timbering was "quite mouldy" in places and the candle was blown out by a draught. "I was going on in the dark, frightened to death, keeping my head down in case I struck the top of the passage." He heard a hissing sound. It was Joe Birkbeck, who hissed as he worked with a pick.

The miners had to work hard to keep up a supply of coal that was picked up by local farmers. They arrived with horses and carts and bought their coal direct at the back-end of the year. They got enough to keep their families warm through a long Dales winter. At peak time, coal was tipped directly into a cart and the charge was for seven hundredweight. They knew roughly how much a wagon could take.

A "coal road" served the bellpits on the high fell between what are now Dent and Garsdale railway stations. The road, once rough and rutted, was metalled after the 1939-45 war. The coal industry flourished from the seventeenth century until the 1870s, when the Settle-Carlisle railway was opened, bringing deep-mined coal from South Yorkshire to the farmsteads and cottages of the upper dales. Mining coal was work for men who could not find a more lucrative job. The thin veins were at an elevation of 1,500 ft. In winter, snow lay on the hills and on the backs of the sheep for weeks on end and a cold wind seemed to put ice in the bloodstream.

A two-handled windlass was fixed to the top of a shaft to lower the workers and to raise the hewn coal. Arriving at his work, a miner sat on a metal bar attached to a rope and was lowered down a shaft up to 120 feet deep. It was a job where a man "dressed down." Fustian trousers with straps around the lower leg were in favour. In confined spaces, they reduced the element of drag. No pumps were avaiilable and the workings were always wet. For his week's labours, a miner would be lucky to earn 15s (75p). From this meagre sum, he was expected to cover the cost of his clothing and equipment – implements, blasting powder and candles.

During the General Strike of 1926, when the nation's main pits closed, an enterprising dalesman took coal from outcrops in the valley of the Greta near Burton-in-Lonsdale to Dent, where there was a coal famine. He should have sold the coal immediately but preferred to bask in the fame his enterprise had brought him. News came through of the end of the strike. Soon the miners would be back at work. The entrepreneur could scarcely give his cart load of coal away.

Tups and Yows

The thirteenth annual Ribblehead Sheep Show had the celebrated railway viaduct and Whernside as a backdrop, Swaledale sheep as the stars, a tentful of produce and handicrafts to be judged, a wooden cow to be "milked" and old friendships to be renewed by day-trippers from places as far apart as Bradford and Swaledale.

Thankfully, the weather was on its best behaviour – warm rather than hot, dry rather than soaking wet, with the sky cloudy-bright rather than laden with clouds the colour of Stephens's blue-black ink. For once, the climate was comfortable and there was clout-casting on a grand scale as the hot conditions persisted.

The event was held, as usual, on land at the back of the Station Inn. A high wall had been "gapped" for the day and would doubtless have been walled up again by dusk. Thanks were extended to "mine host," to Dr J A Farrer, lord of the manor, and to the farmers who had rights of pasturage on Blea Moor. The show was a diversion for the moorland sheep, which normally have only ramblers and train-spotters to observe.

The last show had been marked by teeming precipitation. The railway embankment offered a little protection for the showfield and the inn benefited from having its western gable-end reinforced with corrugated iron. People huddled under the cover of the big tent or adjacent buildings. The sheep, in their pens, had nowhere to go. One man was heard to remark: "I reckon t'day's bin up all neet."

For the latest show, I parked my car on a hard surface near the junction between the Ribblesdale road and the Ingleton-Hawes turnpike – a wild spot indeed. I was early enough to be able to pick a good place. Latecomers parked their cars wherever they could. When the sun shone, it brought a responsive gleam from a couple of hundred vehicles.

I was early enough for the gate-keeper, standing beside a card-table at a strategic position in the narrows between inn and bunkhouse, to worry about giving change for the £10 notes being proferred. In the end, I was nodded through, on the understanding that I would return with a £1 coin at the earliest opportunity. I entered Ribblehead Sheep Show at the concessionary rate for OAPs, which was £1, this figure including the catalogue.

I patronised the refreshment room, where a collection of tasty food was a major stimulant for the saliva glands. Even the scones had become calorific, having been liberally coated with butter. Coffee served hot in a plastic cup immediately quenched the thirst. A friend reminded me of the Dales dance at which a parched dancer had reeled towards one of the windows, had taken the flowers out of a vase and drunk the water in a series of noisy gulps.

The secretary's "tent" was indeed a caravan. Within I could see the gleam of newly-polished silver, from the assembled trophies. It was decreed that "the judge's decision is final, that the committee might withhold any prize money or trophy if they have reasonable cause to do so" and no covers for pens were allowed.

At ten o'clock precisely, the judges began to attend to the local sheep classes. In the catalogue, a "tup" had become the posher "ram." It was a bad time for hill farming, with meagre profits plunging into losses, with lambs being bought at give-away prices and with wood "worth nowt." A man commented grimly: "I reckon we'll hev to start breeding sheep wi'out fleeces." The sheep themselves, oblivious of modern economic conditions, tolerated their brief spell of celebrity after the freedom of the hills.

As the sheep were held in a line for judgement, a young lady from Thirsk, with an impressive photographic outfit, concentrated on getting good close-ups – so close at times I felt that she was making a speciality of the farmers' tonsils. It was a characterful assembly of farmers, most of them lean and lish after their fell-going life. In straitened times, they were not running to fat.

As for me, I had arranged to meet two young men from Leeds who were making a video about Yorkshire and had wanted to start off with something authentically of the Dales. The Ribblehead Sheep Show might have been made for them. As I spoke, the background noises included the bleating of sheep, a child's cry that was suppressed by a multi-coloured dummy, shrill whistles from farmers, the clatter of a passing freight train and the rattle as trailers were opened up to disgorge another lot of sheep on to the showground.

I was also aware of a wash of homely conversations. I asked the cameraman if he had caught any of the farmers' comments. He could only remember one. What on earth did "off t-tops" mean? A farmer who had been listening began to utter wheezy sounds, like that of a swinging gate in need of having its hinges oiled. It then dawned on me that he was – laughing.

For several hours I lived in a world of sheep, farmers, crooks (which I hasten to add are of the type also known as sticks) and Cumberland and Westmorland style wresting. In the open sheep sections were some of the best sheep breeders in the Dales, with entries from as far away as Low Row in Swaledale and Bainbridge in Wensleydale, from Catlow, in the upper valley of the Hodder, and from Coniston, near the heart of the Lake District.

As for the sheep, which were the main reason for the gathering, we were treated to a range of animals with names resonant of the old Norse days. It was a pity that the males were rams, not "tups." What you made of such terms as shear ram, gimmer shearling and mule gimmer lamb distinguished the farming community from the curious townies.

In the marquee were paintings of sheep by children. It reminded me of the art class in a Dales school when a boy from a dalehead farm was having trouble with the sky. The teacher filled in a blue sky with fluffy white clouds. The lad looked disappointed and remarked: "Nay, miss – where I come from t'clouds is mucky."

Wheezing and Wailing

In the wrong hands, a harmonium can be an instrument of torture, bringing tears to the eyes for the wrong reasons and concussing the woodworm. Well-played, it evokes a period in rural Nonconformity of lusty hymn-singing – a time when music had recognisable tunes.

In the tiny chapel at Castle Bolton, in Wensleydale, is a harmonium of American origin. Seeing it reminded me of some research I conducted into the Dales associations of Edward Elgar, one of England's premier composers. In the collection of his friend Charles William Buck was a printed copy of little-known vesper voluntaries for "organ, harmonium or American organ." Elgar had inscribed the copy he gave to Buck.

The surviving Dales harmoniums stand in fretworked splendour, smelling either of foisty hymns books or, if the chapel is still regularly used, of furniture polish. In less than competent hands, a harmonium wheezes and wails. Sometimes the musical accompaniment to the hymn-singing stops abruptly. This happened during the singing of "Fight the good fight." The organist remarked: "Fight's ower. T'cords brokken."

A lady harmoniumist who was playing an unfamiliar piece was asked by the preacher if she could use a more up-to-date tune. She replied: "Tha can't have it more up-to-date than this. I'm making it up as I go on."

One step up from the harmonium is the hand-pumped organ. The organ-blower sat to one side and hoped that he or she who was playing did not become too exuberant during a rousing hymn tune by Charles Wesley. The blower's guide as to how much air was available was indicated by a lead pellet. This dangled from a piece of string that rested against woodwork that had been marked "full" or "empty." At Austick chapel, of blessed memory, someone had marked above "full" the word "bust." The Austwick blower became redundant when the instrument was electrified.

A Methodist local preacher was to have a special memory of the attractive little chapel at Barden, in Upper Wharfedale. The building is now a craft centre. In the chapel days, the downstairs accommodation was the home of the chapel-keeper, who was also the steward, organist and caretaker. She provided a meal for the visiting preacher.

Welcoming the local preacher, she gave him a cup of tea and then directed him up a flight of uncarpeted steps to the vestry. He told me that a hen scuttered up the stairs before him. It was said to lay its eggs in the vestry. Hopefully, its clucking would not destroy the concentration of the preacher. When service time arrived, he entered the chapel proper to find that the one member of the congregation, being hard of hearing, was sitting in the front pew. The lady who had been acting as steward now donned another hat, that of organist. While passing him on her way to the organ, she remarked; "Cut thi sermon short when tha smells t'Yorkshire pudding." He followed her advice and, shortly after the service had ended, he was sitting down to a splendid lunch.

A compact, hi-tech organ, offspring of the American space programme, was bought with a bequest and installed at little Hubberholme church, at the head of Wharfedale. Having such a valuable organ, it was important to keep the ancient church warm. This became known to a rambler who, on a chilly winter day, was known to sneak into the building, here to pray, then sleep.

Among the lost harmoniums of the Dales are two that featured in services held in railway waiting rooms – at Ribblehead and Garsdale – in the days when each place had a strong community of railwaymen and farmers. Both instruments came into their own on Sunday afternoons, when services were conducted by the Vicars of Ingleton and Garsdale respectively.

At Ribblehead, the harmonium stood in a corner of the waiting room and some of those who waited for trains could not resist playing a tune on it.

Owd Ben's Advice

A chap hez nobbut once to live,
He's nobbut once to dee;
His days dahn 'ere are nobbut few
So 'earken lad ta me.

Enjoy thissen woll still tha'rt young
An' dunnot ape t'owd men;
Tha'll be grey an dotin' sooin enuff
Baht doin' it thissen.

Live thi life as best tha can,
Be honest, good and straight,
And if tha follers this advice
Tha'll get ta heaven all reight.

DENNIS PAGE.

110

Billy and Nanny

Goats were not kept on Dales farm for decoration. They dropped their kids early in the year. When the Swaledale sheep were lambing, the nanny goats had enough milk for their offspring and for any weak or "starved" lambs. Old farmers kept a goat in a milk-house when there was a risk of cattle picking [suffering from contagious abortion]. When this did not happen a second time, which was usually the case, the goat got the credit for preventing it.

Dick Metcalfe knew about goats. In the days when his family were at Crackpot Hall, "back o' Kisdon," four nanny goats and a billy had the freedom of the local crags. They had some woodland in which to browse and rock overhangs under which to shelter when the weather was wet and windy. There was no sorrier spectacle than a rain-sodden goat.

A goat would "live off owt." One that was a favourite with day-trippers to a remote Dales inn provided the household and guests with fresh milk. The day-trippers fed the goat with an astonishing variety of edibles, including cigarettes. A pipe-smoker cut a two-inch long piece from his twist tobacco, which was hard and dark, and offered this to the goat, which was said to be so pleased "she fair smacked her lips." The next supply of milk from the goat had a tobacco flavour? When one of the guests said he did not like goat's milk, the landlord whispered to a friend: "He gat it – and didn't knaw."

Tupping time for both goats and sheep was in the autumn. At this time of year, the billy goat at Crackpot Hall roamed far and wide. He was known to reach Tan Hill inn and he also went off down the dale as far as Low Row. The billy's return journey to Crackpot was usually heralded by a telephone call from a fretful gardener at Muker, reporting there was a goat in the garden.

There are no truly wild goats in the Dales. The last of the feral stock that ranged from Kilnsey Crag to Blue Scar above Arncliffe died in the late 1960s. He was a peevish old billy goat. Lads from Arncliffe lassooed him and took him to a fancy dress dance in the village, where the animal's strong smell – it was rutting time – led to an immediate protest.

These Wharfedale goats were handsome goats, being mainly brown and white. Half a dozen little groups inhabited the limestone country, including Kettlewell, Malham, Austwick and Clapham. Mrs John Anson Farrer, of Ingleborough Hall, had a pedigree stud of goats, which were looked after – along with the home farm – by Barton Tomlinson. The Hird family arranged with him to have their best nanny crossed with one of the prize billies. The result was outstanding. The Hirds milked the goats to bottle-feed the lambs. One animal suckled fourteen spare lambs for a short time at the end of a grim winter when the sheep were poor and short of milk.

In due course, the Hird family obtained a billy goat of their own. After the lambing season, the little herd wandered off, invariably to the craggy area near Ingleborough Cave. It was Rob Hird's job to look for them in early spring. "One year, my good friend, our farm lad Ted Lee of Austwick, and myself, had to gather the goats and bring them home. They got into Trow Gill [a ravine flanked by limestone cliffs] and one goat got on to a narrow ledge."

Rob remembered being at one end of the ledge, holding on to a small tree, while Ted – who had a good head for heights – pushed the goat along in front of him. Rob managed to get hold of the horns. "My father went mad when I told him what we had done." When attempts were made to capture a billy-goat at Crackpot Hall, it lost its footing and fell about a hundred feet from the big scar above Kisdon Falls. The animal lived to bleat the tale.

A lamb reared on goat's milk usually had quality and when the time came to sell it, the proud owner usually referred to it as "that goatlamb." Goat kids were lively creatures. They were fond of frolicking on the roofs of farmhouse or outbuildings.

Bill Alderson's father, who farmed at Angram, borrowed a billy goat from Tom (Bosh) Metcalfe of West Stonesdale. Bill, then a lad, was given the job of collecting it, which he did, using a length of cord as a lead. The billy was huge, with a "gurt beard." It was pally [friendly] and, this being the time of the rut, smelly. When Bill entered the farm kitchen after securing the goat his mother said: "Where's ta bin? Smells as though thou's bin in t'lile house" [outside toilet]. Bill was told to strip naked. His clothes were washed.

In North Ribblesdale, my informant was the late lamented Peter Wood, who told me of a time when the upper dale had a herd of about twenty nannies and a billy. It was in a sense a community herd, consisting of goats that belonged to four local families – to the Booths of Nether Lodge, the Masons of Lodge Hall, the Morphets of Birkwith and his own family. The goats summered in and around Ling Gill, where there was a craggy terrain, with woodland and rock crevices for shelter. The animals were gathered and sorted out according to ownership about a month before lambing. They were kept inside and foddered using hay and a few "nuts" to stimulate the milk flow.

In those days a farmer would "croft" sheep. Ewes that were about to lamb were driven into crofts so that they could be supervised at regular intervals during the night. The conscientious farmer would cat-nap on a sofa in the kitchen and be up and about at midnight, then at about 4 a.m. and an hour or two after that. "When he went to the croft to look over the sheep, he'd take a goat on a lead. If he found a 'starved' lamb, he'd give it a drink from the goat. It had milk of the right temperature 'on tap'. When that farmer went out next time, he'd take a fresh goat."

Visiting one farm at the time of the rut, I was gently warned, as I prepared to rub the head of a friendly billy goat, not to touch the area of the scent glands. The Pennine breeze was wafting the smell of billy to where the nannies were kept. They would scream in response.

Fish and Chips

I grew up in Skipton, "gateway to the Dales," in the Hungry Thirties. Fish and chips, from a shop, formed a quick meal costing just a few coppers. This appealed to mothers who must also work in the mills and had little time, inclination or "brass" to prepare fancy food.

My youthful appetite for fish and chips was sharpened by the protracted queuing, during which patience was a necessity and not just a virtue. At meal-times, queues often extended from the shop on to the pavement. The normally silent queue shuffled forward, a few steps at a time, as fry-up succeeded fry-up. A sizzling sound indicated that more fish or a load of chipped potatoes had been placed in the pans.

Grunting and growling might be heard if someone jumped the queue by joining a friend or, in a loud whisper, requested that someone near the front might get some additional fish and chips – for them. The system worked so well because it was based on morality, not self-interest though the youngest children, standing on tiptoe so that they might see above the counter, would wait until the staff had their backs to the customers and then take a quick swig from the vinegar bottle. And every child would wistfully request "some scraps, mister."

It was pleasurable to run home with the fish and chips in their crinkly brown wrapping-paper resting beneath my jumper "to keep them warm." They in turn kept me warm on chilly evenings, though the under-the-jumper treatment did strange things to the shape of the fish, giving them a plaice-like flatness.

Each shop was known for the quality, or otherwise, of its products. At one, t'batter's like armour-plating. Another shopkeeper was stingy with chips. Most shops, in that highly competitive age, provided first-class service and high quality food, though the modern stomach would turn at the sight of a hunk of dripping floating in the pan like an off-white iceberg.

Our Charlie

To watch and listen as Charlie Lawson, of Giggleswick, entertained a compa-
ny of old people or the local Women's Institute was to marvel at his memory
and his stamina. He was never "fast for a word." Charlie was smaller than
average, was mentally adroit and had come close to discovering the secret of
perpetual motion.

Being "good with his hands," he joined the firm of R Haygarth &
Sons, whose speciality was making and repairing cycles. It was not
long before Charlie, having discovered a penny farthing in the back
room, was raising his first local laughs by pedalling up and down
Duke Street on the cumbersome machine.

He told of the man who was seen riding a penny farthing down
Buckhaw Brow in the days before the road was "metalled." The difference between this man and other pioneer cyclists was that he had
his legs over the handlebars. At the bottom of the hill, he explained
to an inquirer: "I've bin chucked over t'handlebars that often, I thowt
that next time I'd land on mi feet."

The late 1920s and early 1930s saw Charlie indulging in another
passion – for motor bikes. The neighbours must have shuddered
whenever they heard him revving up his machine. It was almost certainly one he had built himself from bits and pieces. He and his
friends raced on grass on land near the top of Buckhaw Brow.

A restless Charlie Lawson, feeling hemmed in at work, decided to
emigrate to Canada. He got as far as applying and attending a doctor
for inoculations, but an allergic reaction to these prevented him from
migrating to North America. He shruggled his shoulders, returned to
work – and re-entered his fantasy world via the stage of the Victoria
Hall at Settle.

Came the 1939-45 war. At first, Charlie was a special policeman. His
nightly prowling, in search of any chinks of light from door-edge or

window – chinks that might be seen by enemy aircraft – led to some of his most amusing tales. Noticing light coming from under the doorway of a cottage in upper Settle, he knocked and on entering found an old couple sitting by the fire. "Do you know you have a light showing under your door?" Charlie asked. The old man looked up and said: "Why, they're not coming i' submarines are they?"

Charlie joined the RAF in 1944 and though he trained as an aircraft technician he had soon joyfully joined the ENSA Concert Party, touring the length and breadth of Britain in the course of providing entertainment for the Troops. He had a motor bike, of course, and when he was stationed in Yorkshire he made good use of it at weekends to return to North Ribblesdale and his wife, Gladys, whom he had married in 1942.

On demobilisation, Charlie returned to his old job. Now he was a partner in the enterprise. When Jim Haygarth died in 1959, he took over the business. He sold it to buy property in Church Street, where he developed an antiques business that sustained him and his family when he retired in 1972.

He entertained local organisations with his fund of stories, including that of the motorist who was driving along a country road when a three-legged chicken ran across in front of him and entered a farmyard. Thinking he must have imagined it, but wanting to satisfy his curiosity, he drove into the yard and met the farmer. "Have you seen a three-legged chicken run in here?" "Aye," replied the farmer, "I breed 'em."

The motorist said: "They can't half run. Are they good to eat?" Said the farmer: "I've no idea. I haven't caught one of the little beggers yet."

He was fond of golf – and of telling stories about golf, including that relating to a lady who, looking for a lost golf ball, found it in the middle of a cow-clap. She made an effort to hit the ball. Charlie said this was not allowed, adding: "You're not supposed to hit a ball when it's in motion."

Charlie died in 1984. The last time I met him, he was exercising his dog Mintie in a riverside field. We had an exchange of Yorkshire tales. I reminded Charlie of the one he had told and which had long been a favourite of mine. A man lay in bed. His wife was undressing beside the window. The curtains were drawn back. The bedroom light was burning. Said the husband: "For goodness sake, close those curtains." "Why?" asked the wife. He replied: "I don't want all the neighbours to think I've married you for your money."

Charlie found humorous aspects in the dying process and had told the story of a man who was sitting by his dying wife's bedside when she opened her eyes and said: "If you want to marry again when I've gone, I won't mind, though don't let whoever it is wear my clothes." Said the husband: "Of course not, lass. Anyway, they won't fit her."

Cross All Joints

Americans who visit the Dales are captivated by what one of them called "those cute stone fences." She was referring to the drystone walls that form a futuristic pattern in the villages and climb the fellsides with the devil-may-care attitude of soldiers in battle. An old-time waller remarked: "Every cobble hes its face – but it isn't any fool can find it!"

My father-in-law, a West Craven farmer, was fond of telling the story of how a local waller became known as Moonlight Jack. He was a good waller who gave value for money. He ensured there were good foundations, that the courses were level, joints were crossed, plenty of "through stones" were used to bind the two sides of a wall together and the capstones fitted snugly. When he reached a stage where there were no gapped walls left in the district he would go out on a moonlit night and pull down a few stretches to keep himself in employment.

I have been heartened in recent years to see that the ancient skills of walling have not been forgotten. A national drystone walling association has keen supporters in Yorkshire. At summertime shows, like Kilnsey, walling competitions are well- supported and also provide visitors with abiding interest. One lad who was not making a reight good job of his section said, ruefully: "They'd better judge it quick – or it'll tummel down."

Tommy Chapman, of Buckden, a farm man who spent a good half of his time gap-walling told me, long years ago, that "a good waller goes by t'rack o' t'eye and doesn't pick t'same bit o' stone up twice." Because no two stones were alike, the work was never monotonous. If a wall was put up reight, it'd last a lifetime.

"A lot o' farmers don't seem to take time with the walls. They just throw 'em up any way." He'd heard that most of the walls around Buckden had been built as part-time work for the lead-miners. They had received about a shilling a day for their efforts.

Some relatively new walls and the remains of ancient boundaries are seen by those who walk along a lane near Malham youth hostel. The lane leads to a "clapper" bridge across the beck that flows from the letterbox cavity at the base of Malham Cove. A local farmer pointed to the steep area where the fields are small. He said it was an old dodge for a chap who wished to sell stock to take the potential buyer on the low side. Cattle looked bigger when viewed from below. When this dalehead landscape was cleared of rubble, there was more than enough stone for walling. The rest was made into neat heaps. One Malham waller was said to be so speedy he'd work for a day – and it took him two days to get back home!

A drystone wall divides up the land. When new land was being taken in from the moor, the wall provided a prominent demarcation and behind it the land could be improved, sweetened by lime and fertilised by cow-claps and sheep droppings. So moor became rough pastureland and some of the rough pastureland became meadows from which sun and wind-dried grass could be taken as hay, fodder for the wintering stock.

A mortarless wall also provides bield [shelter] for the sheep. When a wind full of spite lashes a hill farm with rain, sheep find a snug, dry retreat at the lee side of a wall. The wind might whistle between the stones but the rain stays on the other side. Notice, as you tour the Dales, that short stretches of wall stand by themselves on open ground. These are bield-walls that break the back of the wind for cattle or sheep that lie behind them.

Where a wall climbs the steep side of a hill, as on the "nose end" of Penyghent, notice how the builder has kept all the courses level. It would be folly to angle them according to the contours. Notice, too, how our drystone walls are a ready guide to local geology. The old-time wallers did not carry stones further than was necessary. Buckhaw Brow, near Settle, is on the line of a geological fault, with limestone on one side of the road and gritstone on the other. The transition from one type of rock to another is evident by looking at the walls that flank the road. On some stretches the pearl-white of limestone is cheek-by-jowl with the warm brown of gritstone.

Maintaining a limestone wall is no easy task. Limestone might be so rough on the hands, they would bleed if gloves were not worn. At a wall-end, left where there is a gateway or where the land of one person was adjacent to that of another, it is seen that in reality a Dales wall is two walls in one, situated side by side, held together by long flattish stones known as "throughs." Small stones form the packing.

A row of capstones helps to protect the wall. A typical wall is four feet wide at the bottom, tapering to two and a-half feet. The tapering is known as the "batter." If a gap occurs, the material for repair is readily to hand. For a time, the wall might be "singled" to prevent stock from straying.

Many stretches of wall incorporate what is known in Craven as a "cripple 'oil" and in some other areas as a "creep." This permits mixed grazing, restraining cows but allowing sheep to enter adjacent land. Another time, it allowed a farmer to drive sheep being "gathered" on a more direct course, avoiding the opening and closing of gates. A large piece of slate is available to block the gap as necessary.

The cripple 'oil at one farm was unusually large, being able to accommodate a donkey, with inches to spare. The donkey in question did not like being ridden. If someone climbed on its back, it made straight for the hole. The rider had only seconds to dismount before hitting the wall. The other day, in Settle, I saw a Dales farmer eyeing up a badly-damaged Land Rover. He said to the owner: "Has ta bin trying to get through a cripple 'oil?"

A Wharfedale man remembers when a couple o' Scotch tups met in t'middle of a cripple 'oil. It was tupping time. They backed, on either side of the hole, and then they "set to." There was a heck of a bang in the middle. "They didn't upset t'wall – it were well built – but by gow what a crack!"

That Wharfedale chap, looking back on his walling experience, says: A lot of t'stone was aw right. You did get odd parts where t'stone wasn't all that good. Sandstone stuff (we called it 'greet') was not bad to wall wi'. So was a lot of t'limestone if there were sharp bits on it. It were not so bad if you got some decent stone. If you came to an area where you were bothered w' a lot o' little bits, you put a heck of a lot of stones on t'wall and didn't git ower far. You got a lot o' shapes and sizes but they fit in with one another. You wanted 'em rough-edged so they'd bite in.

Limestone was smoother than sandstone but played heck wi' your fingers. I knew a fellow as worked wi' us walling limestone up t'dale who walled till he was leaving red fingerprints on t'stone. We said: "Now, come on, give ower." But he was there next day. He came wi' a pad of leather on each hand and he kept going…He was a hard man.

Some stuff we used at Hazlewood and Storiths looked as though it'd come out of t'river bottom. It was hard stuff, like granite. It'd bin smoothed over wi' watter at some time. You try and wall wi' them things – oh, man! I put a gap up for an owd-fashioned farmer – by gum, he was an old stager – and I'd a heck of a job to keep it up. I told him it was bad stuff to wall wi'. He said: "Thou mun excuse me for saying so, Geordie, but it looks as thou t'damn pigs has been at it." I said: "If thou gits any pigs near this, it'll be down again." It stood, seemingly.

When I was walling a lile bit, in t'nineteen forties, such work was included in a farm man's wage. There was no such thing as an eight-hour day. You worked as lang as there was any dayleet. I spent some time in East Lancs. We had some Lonk sheep – big, upstanding, horned sheep – and they were belters for jumping walls. A sheep 'ud back-back, take a few steps and clear a wall just like a deer. You could-n't hod them things at any price.

In places, rabbits used to live in walls. I've getten 'em out of a wall two at a time. You had to be rayther careful which way it was facing, cos a rabbit'll nip if it's cornered. I was nipped once when I put my hand in. Then I waited till it got itself turned round afore I got hold of it again.

A Deer Hunt

Robert de Hode, alias Robin Hood, a celebrated slayer of the king's deer, was a Yorkshireman, born in Wakefield. Before he became an outlaw in Barnsdale Forest, in South Yorkshire, he was a juvenile delinquent, charged with stealing some firewood. At least, that's my story – and I'm sticking to it. What about the wild red deer of the Yorkshire Dales?

Red deer, inseparably linked with the feudal period, were too large and conspicuous to survive in a free-ranging state when that age had passed. The last of the native red deer of Wharfedale were kept in a park on North Scar, sometimes called The Nab, which lay on the north side of the river, within the Bolton Abbey estate. They were last seen in the 1930s. Eric Foster, a Hellifield farmer, introduced some South Country park reds to his land. They came courtesy of British Railways and when released from the wagons dashed hither and thither. Eric, on horseback, soon managed to round them up.

To visit Eric was to enter a world that seemed remote in spirit from the turbulence of modern life. His farm lay at the end of a long lane that had its beginnings in a maze of little roads near Long Preston church. There were one or two gates to open. The lane served several farms and his was the last.

I remember him introducing the red deer as a whim and because he thought they would make the area more attractive. A fine stockman, he ensured that they would remain in the appointed field and when being moved to pastures new would go through a gate which he would open for them. Not for Eric the flighty type of deer that simply leapt over the walls. He asked their opinion about whether a change was due and would whisper to them at a range of a few feet!

When the time came for me to depart, Eric usually announced a prayer meeting. His dogs prepared for it by sitting on the flagstone steps of a field stile and when he said "Let us pray" each dog bowed its head. The deer were usually some way off. On his leaving the farm, there was a round-up and cull but some of the animals survived. One became the Muckle [great] Stag o' Giggleswick, finding a snug retreat in a gill on Field Gate Farm. A friend who disturbed it photographed the Muckle Stag with a background provided by – Ingleborough!

The first red deer would venture into the Dales some six thousand years ago, when the countryside was becoming clothed with trees and grasses after the million-year-long extravaganza known as the Ice Age. Already there had been reindeer in the area. They summered on the mossy tundra and fell back into wooded areas further south for the winter.

The last native stags in Wharfedale were slain in the early 1930s. They and some hinds had been too venturesome, straying from the old deer park on the hill into the deciduous woods by the Wharfe, a move that made sense to the deer but infuriated the foresters. Red stags have a habit of bole-scoring trees or browsing the foliage. The last of the red deer were shot and the heads of the stags sent to a taxidermist for mounting, the eyes being replaced by amber glass. Thirteen red deer heads survived at Bolton Hall until it was decided to carry out modifications to the room in which they were exhibited. Two heads were retained and the rest given to interested people. No one put a label on the last stag to die.

It was certainly not the stag portrayed by Landseer, Queen Victoria's favourite artist, who was invited by the Duke of Devonshire to provide him with a painting of Bolton Abbey. Landseer arrived to make sketches. He stood out mainly because he wore a maroon velvet shooting coat. He set his easel in the shallows of the River Wharfe and made numerous sketches. The finished painting disappointed the Duke for, entitled "Bolton Abbey in the Olden Time," it was a nondescript interior, with the Abbot (his head based on sketches made of Landseer's friend, Sir Augustus Calcot) making note of dues in kind received from the peasantry – a red stag (with an indifferent head), fish on a platter and a bird that looks astonishing like a bittern.

The Duke who commissioned the work was reconciled to the painting not by its content, which is not what he requested, but by its immense success as a painting. The present Duchess of Devonshire, who sees the painting most days, for it hangs in the entrance hall at Chatsworth, once described it as "an unlikely bag from a very strange day's shooting."

Many years ago, when I decided to go on a Bolton Abbey deer hunt, I saw only two of the mounted heads of Bolton Abbey stock. One adorned the inside of the Rectory, then used by the estate agent. Another was attached to the wall at Barden Tower which, appropriately, was a hunting lodge of some of the dukal forebears – the Cliffords of Skipton and Bolton – who owned the Forest of Barden.

Today, at Chatsworth, the principal home of the Duke and Duchess of Devonshire, both red and fallow deer languish under ancient oaks in the Old Park. At Bolton Abbey, the roe deer, as insubstantial as a shadow, flits through the woods. If you stand outside the Devonshire Arms, you will see two deer – on the family's coat of arms.

T'Owd Ways

When I met Tommy Moore of Hawes, I discovered he was clinging to as much of the old Dales routine as he could. He was hand-milking cows while, at the Dales Countryside Museum a short distance down the road, the process was being evoked with dummies and farming bygones.

Tommy, a bachelor, was commuting between his double-fronted house on the main street a matter of a few hundred yards to some out-buildings and land beside the Gayle road. He used a Massey-Ferguson tractor, one of his concessions to a modern way of farming. Tommy was up and about early to hand-milk a dozen cows. He was breeding all his own stock and had "followers" of various ages.

This was farming as it used to be. Hay was fed to the cows from a fodder-gang. As he sat on the traditional three-legged stool to milk the cows, he had to beware of the swish of a tail, especially if there were any "muck-buttons," those bits of dried dung that might inflict painful cuts. Two hazards at milking time are the proness of a restless cow to kick over the bucket used for the milk – and the cow-pat process that begins when the animal lifts its tail.

I was reminded of a third hazard, as told to me by a Dales vet. He attended a sick cow and anaesthetised it, sticking the needle into the cow again to assure himself that it had taken effect. The farmer, highly impressed, asked to borrow the needle. He looked at it for a few moments, then impulsively stuck it into the leg of another cow, which lashed out with the leg. The farmer bounced off the shippon wall.

The hand-milker turns his cap so that the neb is at the back. He presses his head into the flanks of the cow as his fingers rhythmically massage the teats and bring forth spurts of milk that make a distinctive sound on the sides of the pail. When the milking process was over, Tommy had to go through the old routine of "mucking out." He was born at "Haas," as the native pronounces the name of the upper

Wensleydale market town. When he left school he went to work for a local farmer, John Metcalfe (who was nicknamed Jackie Buller) for 14s.6d a week, which included his keep. "Me and Kit Lambert worked there about thirty years." They milked maybe seven cows each, twice a day. "It's a knack. In winter we stuck a candle on a window-ledge so that we could see what we were doing." In 1966, when the boss died, the two men took over the farm. "Kit died – and now there's only me. I have a lad who works for me a bit." In the old days, he milked Shorthorn cattle. At haytime, he was "scrattin' wi' hosses and hand-rakes. We mowed all t'wallsides wi' scythes. It was a matter of getting every bit of hay you could manage." The memories of a half-forgotten Dales life spilled out of Tommy's mind. We grimaced at the thought of muck-spreading by hand – of loading a horse-drawn cart with muck at the midden and distributing it in neat little heaps, from which it was "scaled" or spread, using a fork. "It was a back-breaking job."

There were concessions to modernity. He was milking Friesians, the successors of Shorthorns and Ayrshires that once bedecked the fields of the Dales and were in-wintered, many of them in outbarns that dot the landscape. His buildings were connected to the national electricity grid. Milk was not being cooled and poured into kits but flowed into a refrigerated tank for collection by a vehicle from Hawes Creamery (which stands just across the road from Tommy buildings). The milk from Tommy's cattle was making a small but important contribution to the production of the dale's most famous product – Wensleydale cheese.

As we parted, I remarked: "To sum it up – you've managed to stick to the old ways and show a profit." Tommy grinned. "Not last year. It was a disaster…"

Farmhouse Christmas

It will be a lean Christmas on many Dales farms. The slump in prices for stock affects even quite large milk producers and wool prices have slumped so much that it has cost more to employ a man to shear a sheep than can be recovered by the sale of the wool. In these straitened times, a farmer about to buy a computer pondered for a while and said: "I think I'll buy a chair instead. Then I can sit and watch t'cows. I'm on t'spot if there's owt amiss."

On the first Christmas, the drama surrounding the birth of Christ took place in a stable in the presence of oxen. Many of the greetings cards we receive are of the Nativity and give the stable a cosy appearance. The Dales equivalent of that stable would be an outbarn or mistal, which Arnold Kellett, in a Christmas poem written in the West Riding dialect, described as "shabby and bare, all stinking wi' cow muck." The poem ends with a reference to "a lass wi' 'er babby, all snuggled in t'ay."

The legacy of the frantic years, when "thou's got to run to stand still," is seen in farm buildings that Alan Bennett, who has a home in the Dales, compared with aircraft hangers. Once herby meadows are growing wall-to-wall silage grass. Few dairy cattle remain in the upper dales. Dales outbarns are deserted and forlorn, yet within living memory farm children, following field paths on their way to school, would call at them in turn to fodder the stock. Their parents would follow-up, watering the animals and "mucking-out." The Hawes rope-maker made cow-bands, which were used when a cow spending the winter in a stall was tied up loosely by the neck. I have marvelled at the docility of the domestic cow.

"Brass" was in short supply when the oldest amang us were kids in the Dales. One recalls a farmer who, in frugal mood, said: "I'm bahn to have all t'family up for a reight good meal just before Christmas. I'm not buying toys for t'kids. They'll nobbut break 'em."

Edith Carr, who lived at a farm on Malham Moor, recalls that just before Christmas she and her children went out looking for a small conifer tree of a suitable size to be decorated for the Christmas season. A tree was found and set up in the living room, where decorations from former years, and small gifts recently purchased, adorned its branches. The tree also had small candles in clip-on metal holders. As she went out to milk the cows, Edith told her children not to light any of the candles when she was not present.

She had not been milking for long when a child rushed into the shippon to report that the Christmas tree had set on fire. One of the children had lit a candle. The startled mother was told: "Don't worry – we've put the fire out." How had they done it? A large jug of milk stood on the nearby table. They poured the milk over the flaming branches. That Christmas, the pungent smell of burnt milk tainted the air in every room of the house.

> *Here's ti thoo, an' all 'at's thahn,*
> *Here's ti me, an' all 'at's mahn,*
> *Maay all t'good luck, 'at luck can send,*
> *Be thahn an' mahn reeght up ti' t'end –*
> *Is what Ah wish, an' what Ah pray*
> *Ti leeght on all this Kessemas Daay.*

Some Recent Castleberg Books
by W R Mitchell

Birds of the Lake District

This new-style bird book is for the many visitors to the Lake District who are attracted by the birds of mountain, lake or shore and would like to know more about them and their places in England's most astonishing tract of country. The book supplements the standard handbook on birds by concentrating on the most distinctive species. The author, Bill Mitchell, has studied local bird life for over half a century. The illustrator, David Binns, is one of our finest bird artists.

ISBN: 1 871064 64 3 £6.50

Cuckoo Town
Dales Life in the 1950s

When the future state of the countryside is being hotly debated, we look back at life in Austwick in the middle of the 20th century when a well-balanced community found contentment in life that is not to be experienced in the brash, media-led world of today. Every page has its tales of characters who lived in the Yorkshire Dales of not-so-long-ago.

ISBN: 1 871064 59 7 £6.50

One Hundred Tales of the Settle-Carlisle Railway

From many tape-recordings, made over a spell of thirty years, Bill Mitchell selects anecdotes that capture the spirit of the Settle-Carlisle, our most celebrated railway. Read about Hangman's Hut and the ghost of the Whistling Soldier; also about the signalman who was marooned for three days and three nights. The book is extremely well illustrated. Foreword by Ann Cryer, MP.

ISBN: 1 871064 49 X   £6.99

Other Castleberg Titles

Birds of the Yorkshire Dales	£6.50
Ghost-hunting in the Yorkshire Dales	£5.99
Music of the Yorkshire Dales	£5.99
Sacred Places of the Lake District	£6.50
Beatrix Potter – Her Life in the Lake District	£6.20
The Lost Village of Mardale	£5.60
Garsdale – History of a Junction Station	£6.50
Mile by Mile on the Settle to Carlisle	£5.99
The Men Who Made the Settle to Carlisle	£5.99
Life in the Lancashire Milltowns	£5.99
Nowt's Same	£6.50
You're Only Old Once	£4.99

Mini biographies:

Tot Lord and the Bone Caves	£4.50
Edith Carr – Life on Malham Moor	£4.50
Edward Elgar in the Yorkshire Dales	£4.99
Fred Taylor: Yorkshire Cheesemaker	£4.99

All **Castleberg** titles are available at good bookshops or,
in case of difficulty, please write to:
North Yorkshire Marketing, 22 Azerley Grove,
Harrogate, North Yorkshire HG3 2SY
We will be pleased to send you a complete list of titles
and an order form
No postage is charged on **Castleberg** books